The 5 Ingredients Mediterranean Diet Cookbook for Beginners:

2000 Days of Quick & Easy 30-Minute Recipes with a 4-Week Meal Plan for Healthy Eating & Weight Loss

Copyright © 2025 Helen Robbins
All rights reserved.

No part of this book may be copied, reproduced, stored in a retrieval system, or transmitted in any form or by any means—electronic, mechanical, photocopying, recording, or otherwise—without prior written permission from the author or publisher, except for brief quotes in reviews. Unauthorized distribution or reproduction of this book is a violation of copyright law.

Disclaimer

The information provided in this book is for educational and informational purposes only. The author and publisher are not medical professionals, nutritionists, or dietitians. This cookbook does not intend to diagnose, treat, or cure any medical condition. Readers should consult with a qualified healthcare provider before making any significant dietary or lifestyle changes, especially if they have existing health conditions, food allergies, or are pregnant or nursing.

While every effort has been made to ensure the accuracy of the information in this book, the author and publisher assume no responsibility for errors, omissions, or outcomes resulting from the use of recipes, meal plans, or dietary suggestions. Any reliance placed on the information in this book is strictly at the reader's own risk.

The nutritional values provided for each recipe are estimates and may vary based on portion size, ingredient brands, and cooking methods. Always verify nutritional content based on your dietary needs.

The Mediterranean diet is a lifestyle-based approach to eating and wellness. Individual results may vary, and this book does not guarantee weight loss or specific health outcome.

Table of Contents

Introduction 5
Welcome to the Mediterranean Lifestyle 5
The Power of Five 5
Why five ingredients? 5

Mediterranean Pantry Essentials 6
Stocking Your Mediterranean Pantry 6
Oils & Vinegars: The Heart of Mediterranean Cooking 6
Herbs & Spices: The Secret to Bold Mediterranean Flavors 7
Proteins: Lean, Nutrient-Rich, and Satisfying 7
Fresh Produce: The Soul of Mediterranean Cuisine 8
Bringing It All Together 8
How to Start Cooking with These Essentials: 8

Breakfast Bliss 9
Greek Yogurt with Chia, Almonds & Berries 9
Mediterranean Tomato & Feta Scramble 9
Mediterranean Chia Seed Pudding 10
Air-Fried Zucchini & Egg Frittata 10
Mediterranean Almond Flour Pancakes 11
Avocado & Egg Mediterranean Wrap 11
Mediterranean Chia Pudding with Berries 12
Cucumber & Labneh Breakfast Bowl 12
Air-Fried Mediterranean Apple Rings 13
Mediterranean Fig & Almond Smoothie 13
Cinnamon-Spiced Quinoa Breakfast Bowl 14
Air-Fried Sweet Potato & Egg Hash 14
Cottage Cheese & Fig Bowl 15
Mediterranean Pear & Ricotta Bowl 15
Scrambled Eggs with Sun-Dried Tomatoes & Basil 16
Greek Yogurt & Pistachio Bowl 16
Baked Ricotta with Honey & Nuts 17
Air-Fried Halloumi & Tomato Bites 17
Mediterranean Lemon & Honey Porridge 18
Dark Chocolate & Walnut Overnight Oats 18

Satisfying Salads 19
Cucumber & Dill Yogurt Salad 19
Avocado & Cherry Tomato Salad 19
Mediterranean Chickpea & Cucumber Salad 20
Roasted Beet & Walnut Salad 20
Cabbage & Apple Slaw 21
Roasted Pepper & Feta Salad 21
Cabbage & Carrot Slaw with Lemon Dressing 22
Arugula & Walnut Salad with Lemon Zest 22
Mediterranean Tomato & Basil Salad 23
Zucchini & Mint Salad with Yogurt Dressing 23
Roasted Cauliflower & Chickpea Salad 24
Avocado & Roasted Tomato Salad 24
Arugula & Roasted Red Pepper Salad 25
Warm Lentil & Carrot Salad 25
Radish & Fennel Crunch Salad 26
Spinach & Roasted Almond Salad 26
Cucumber, Dill & Feta Salad 27
Roasted Carrot & Chickpea Salad 27
Chickpea & Caper Mediterranean Salad 28
Grilled Zucchini & Halloumi Salad 28

Snacks & Small Plates 29
Olive & Caper Tapenade 29
Baked Feta with Tomatoes 29
Fava Bean & Mint Dip 30
Mediterranean Tuna & White Bean Salad 30
Stuffed Mini Peppers with Hummus 31
Zucchini Chips with Garlic & Oregano 31
Air-Fried Eggplant Chips with Lemon Zest 32
Marinated Artichoke & Olive Skewers 32
Roasted Red Pepper & Walnut Dip 33
Grilled Mushroom & Thyme Bites 33
Lemon & Herb Marinated Feta Cubes 34
Spinach & Cheese Bites 34
Stuffed Dates with Almond Butter 35
Air-Fried Zucchini Parmesan Bites 35
Marinated Cherry Tomatoes with Basil 36
Stuffed Grape Leaves with Lemon & Herbs 36
Crispy Zucchini & Parmesan Bites 37
Eggplant & Chickpea Patties 37
Zesty Carrot & Cumin Dip 38
Air-Fried Stuffed Mushrooms 38
Roasted Red Pepper & Garlic Dip 39
Zucchini Fritters with Dill 39

Quick & Easy Main Dishes 40
Lemon Garlic Shrimp with Zucchini Noodles 40
Garlic & Herb Turkey Meatballs 40
Mediterranean Lentil & Spinach Stir-Fry 41
One-Pan Mediterranean Turkey Skillet 41
Mediterranean Stuffed Bell Peppers 42
Mediterranean Baked Cod with Lemon & Herbs 42
Chickpea & Spinach Stir-Fry 43
Garlic & Herb Grilled Chicken Breasts 43
Roasted Eggplant & Tomato Stew 44
Garlic Lemon Shrimp with Zucchini Noodles 44
Greek-Style Baked Chicken Thighs 45
Mediterranean Lentil & Spinach Stir-Fry 45
Grilled Salmon with Olive Tapenade 46
Balsamic Glazed Chicken & Mushrooms 46
Spiced Turkey & Zucchini Skillet 47
Mediterranean Duck with Cherry Sauce 47
Zucchini & Chickpea Stew 48
Roasted Eggplant & Tahini Bowl 48

Stuffed Peppers with Tuna & Olives 49
Chickpea & Egg Skillet...49

Flavorful Side Dishes 50

Roasted Garlic Green Beans 50
Lemon & Thyme Roasted Carrots 50
Sautéed Zucchini with Garlic & Oregano............ 51
Mediterranean Roasted Bell Peppers 51
Ingredient Mediterranean Quinoa & Parsley Salad
....52
Cumin-Spiced Roasted Cauliflower...................... 52
Roasted Cherry Tomatoes with Basil................... 53
Lemon & Garlic Roasted Brussels Sprouts.......... 53
Roasted Brussels Sprouts with Balsamic Glaze... 54
Sweet Potatoes with Paprika 54
Roasted Fennel with Lemon & Olive Oil 55
Sautéed Swiss Chard with Garlic & Pine Nuts 55
Roasted Red Onion with Balsamic & Thyme....... 56
Warm Mediterranean Tomato & Olive Salad 56
Roasted Eggplant & Garlic Mash 57
Mediterranean Roasted Peppers & Olives 57
Roasted Pumpkin with Cinnamon & Honey........ 58
Air-Fried Cauliflower with Paprika 58
Grilled Zucchini with Basil & Parmesan 59
Sautéed Mushrooms with Thyme 59

Sweet Mediterranean Treats 60

Honey & Orange Yogurt Parfait 60
Baked Cinnamon Apple Slices 60
Dark Chocolate & Pistachio Bites 61
Mediterranean Almond & Date Energy Balls...... 61
Apricot & Sesame Bites....................................... 62
Chia & Coconut Pudding 62

Roasted Pears with Cinnamon & Almonds........... 63
Orange & Olive Oil Mini Muffins 63
Pomegranate & Honey Glazed Figs.....................64
Dark Chocolate-Dipped Apricots..........................64
Honey & Cinnamon Baked Apples.......................65
Dark Chocolate & Almond Energy Bites 65
Greek Yogurt & Honey Parfait 66
Pomegranate & Dark Chocolate Clusters 66
Almond & Fig Bars...67
Citrus & Honey Drizzled Ricotta.........................67
Coconut & Date Truffles......................................68
Chilled Watermelon & Mint Delight 68
Honey & Almond Clusters 69
Grilled Peaches with Ricotta & Honey 69

Simple Mediterranean Meal Plans: 2000 Days of Inspiration 70

The Power of a 4-Week Mediterranean Meal Plan
....70
Week 1 71
Week 2 72
Week 3 73
Week 4 74
Tips for Quick Meal Prep.....................................75

Conclusion 76

The Beauty of Simplicity 76
Embracing the Mediterranean Lifestyle Beyond the
Kitchen 76
Final Words: Your Mediterranean Journey Starts
Now 77

Introduction

Welcome to the Mediterranean Lifestyle

The Mediterranean diet is more than just a way of eating—it's a way of living. Rooted in the time-honored culinary traditions of Greece, Italy, Spain, and surrounding coastal regions, this diet is celebrated for its balance of taste, nutrition, and simplicity. It is no surprise that people in Mediterranean countries enjoy longer lifespans and lower rates of chronic diseases such as heart disease, diabetes, and obesity.

At the heart of the Mediterranean lifestyle is a focus on whole, fresh, and natural ingredients. Olive oil, vibrant vegetables, lean proteins, whole grains, and an abundance of herbs and spices create meals that are not only nourishing but also deeply satisfying. Instead of processed foods and artificial flavors, Mediterranean cuisine thrives on the natural taste of fresh produce, quality fats, and aromatic herbs.

Beyond food, the Mediterranean way of life emphasizes mindful eating, community, and an appreciation for simple pleasures. Meals are often shared with family and friends, enjoyed slowly, and paired with laughter and good conversation. This book invites you to embrace not just the diet, but the entire Mediterranean ethos—one that promotes health, joy, and a more fulfilling relationship with food.

The Power of Five

One of the biggest misconceptions about cooking healthy meals is that it requires a long list of ingredients and hours in the kitchen. The *5 Ingredients Mediterranean Diet Cookbook* proves otherwise. With just five carefully selected ingredients, you can prepare flavorful, nutritious, and satisfying meals without the overwhelm.

Why five ingredients?

- **Simplicity:** Cooking should be enjoyable, not complicated. With fewer ingredients, meal prep is faster, cooking is easier, and cleanup is minimal.
- **Less Waste:** A shorter ingredient list means you use what you buy, reducing food waste and saving money.
- **More Flavor:** With a focus on high-quality, fresh ingredients, every dish bursts with natural flavors that don't need unnecessary additives or fillers.
- **Balanced Nutrition:** Each recipe is designed to provide the essential nutrients needed to fuel your body while keeping calories in check.

By embracing minimalism in cooking, you'll find that a handful of ingredients can create bold and vibrant dishes. Whether you are new to the Mediterranean diet or looking for simple ways to maintain a healthy lifestyle, this cookbook will make nutritious meals effortless and enjoyable.

So, let's get started! With the power of five, you'll discover that eating well doesn't have to be complicated—it just has to be delicious.

Mediterranean Pantry Essentials

The foundation of any great dish starts with the right ingredients. When it comes to Mediterranean cuisine, having a well-stocked pantry ensures that you can create flavorful, nutritious meals with ease—without the need for long and complicated shopping lists. The beauty of the Mediterranean diet is that it relies on fresh, wholesome ingredients that bring natural vibrancy to your plate, making every meal both satisfying and nourishing.

This chapter will guide you through the essential ingredients to keep in your kitchen, focusing on oils and vinegars, herbs and spices, proteins, and fresh produce. With just a handful of these ingredients, you'll be able to prepare a wide variety of delicious Mediterranean dishes that stay true to the *5-ingredient philosophy*—simple, quick, and bursting with flavor.

Stocking Your Mediterranean Pantry

A well-stocked Mediterranean pantry is built on a balance of **heart-healthy fats, aromatic herbs, quality proteins, and fresh seasonal produce**. These core ingredients create the backbone of Mediterranean cooking, allowing you to mix and match effortlessly while maintaining authenticity and nutrition.

Oils & Vinegars: The Heart of Mediterranean Cooking

Mediterranean cuisine revolves around **high-quality olive oil**, which serves as both a cooking fat and a finishing touch for salads, grilled vegetables, and even baked goods. Alongside olive oil, vinegars add depth and brightness to dishes, balancing flavors beautifully.

- **Extra Virgin Olive Oil (EVOO)** – The golden standard of Mediterranean cooking. Rich in heart-healthy monounsaturated fats, EVOO is used for everything from sautéing to salad dressings.
- **Red Wine Vinegar** – A staple for Mediterranean vinaigrettes, marinades, and tangy sauces.
- **Balsamic Vinegar** – Aged and slightly sweet, this vinegar enhances roasted vegetables, meats, and salads.
- **Lemon Juice** – Though technically a fresh ingredient, lemon juice acts as a natural acid replacement for vinegar in many dishes.

How to Use: Drizzle EVOO over roasted vegetables, blend red wine vinegar into a simple dressing, or add balsamic vinegar to caramelized onions for a deep, rich flavor.

Herbs & Spices: The Secret to Bold Mediterranean Flavors

Mediterranean cuisine thrives on **fresh and dried herbs**, enhancing dishes without the need for heavy sauces or excessive salt. These herbs and spices elevate simple ingredients, giving them a distinct and aromatic taste.

- **Oregano** – Earthy and slightly peppery, oregano is a staple for meats, salads, and roasted vegetables.
- **Basil** – Sweet and fragrant, perfect for tomato-based dishes, pestos, and fresh salads.
- **Rosemary** – Adds a woody, aromatic note to roasted potatoes, meats, and baked breads.
- **Thyme** – Subtle and earthy, pairs well with fish, poultry, and legumes.
- **Cumin** – Warm and slightly smoky, often used in Mediterranean stews and spice blends.
- **Paprika** – Sweet or smoked, paprika adds depth to meats, grains, and vegetable dishes.
- **Garlic (Fresh & Powdered)** – Essential in nearly every Mediterranean dish, from sauces to marinades.
- **Cinnamon** – Surprisingly common in Mediterranean cooking, used in stews, roasted vegetables, and desserts.

How to Use: Sprinkle oregano over a Greek salad, add cumin to chickpea dishes, or roast carrots with cinnamon for a sweet-savory twist.

Proteins: Lean, Nutrient-Rich, and Satisfying

Unlike diets that rely heavily on red meat, the Mediterranean diet emphasizes **plant-based proteins, seafood, and lean meats**. These proteins provide the necessary fuel for your body while keeping meals light and heart-healthy.

- **Legumes (Chickpeas, Lentils, Beans)** – Affordable, protein-packed, and fiber-rich, legumes are the backbone of many Mediterranean meals.
- **Fish (Salmon, Sardines, Tuna, Cod)** – Rich in omega-3 fatty acids, seafood is a major protein source in Mediterranean cuisine.
- **Chicken & Turkey** – Lean, versatile, and easy to pair with fresh herbs and citrus.
- **Eggs** – A quick, protein-packed option for breakfast, lunch, or dinner.
- **Greek Yogurt** – A protein powerhouse that also adds creaminess to both savory and sweet dishes.
- **Cheese (Feta, Halloumi, Parmesan)** – While used in moderation, cheese adds a salty, creamy depth to Mediterranean recipes.

How to Use: Whip up a chickpea salad, bake salmon with olive oil and lemon, or scramble eggs with fresh herbs for a quick Mediterranean-inspired meal.

Fresh Produce: The Soul of Mediterranean Cuisine

Fresh, seasonal produce is at the heart of Mediterranean cooking. **Colorful vegetables and fruits** not only provide essential vitamins and fiber but also make every meal naturally vibrant and flavorful.

- **Tomatoes** – Juicy and rich in antioxidants, tomatoes are used in everything from sauces to salads.
- **Cucumbers** – Crisp and refreshing, often paired with yogurt or feta cheese.
- **Bell Peppers** – Sweet and crunchy, perfect for roasting, stuffing, or slicing into salads.
- **Zucchini & Eggplant** – Versatile, mild vegetables that absorb flavors beautifully.
- **Spinach & Arugula** – Nutrient-dense greens for salads, sautés, or omelets.
- **Onions & Garlic** – The flavor base for countless Mediterranean recipes.
- **Citrus (Lemons & Oranges)** – Essential for marinades, dressings, and refreshing desserts.
- **Berries & Grapes** – Naturally sweet, they complement yogurt, salads, and whole-grain dishes.

How to Use: Toss cucumbers and tomatoes with olive oil and feta for a classic Mediterranean salad, roast eggplant with garlic and thyme, or blend citrus into a simple vinaigrette.

Bringing It All Together

With just these pantry staples, you can **create an endless variety of Mediterranean dishes** while staying true to the *5-ingredient concept*. The key to Mediterranean cooking isn't complexity—it's about choosing **high-quality ingredients and letting their natural flavors shine**.

How to Start Cooking with These Essentials:

1. **Mix & Match:** A handful of core ingredients can be combined in different ways for fresh, exciting meals.
2. **Emphasize Simplicity:** A drizzle of olive oil, a squeeze of lemon, and a sprinkle of herbs can transform basic ingredients into something extraordinary.
3. **Keep it Fresh:** While pantry staples provide the foundation, incorporating seasonal produce ensures variety and maximum flavor.

By keeping your kitchen stocked with these essentials, you'll always have what you need to whip up a healthy, flavorful Mediterranean meal—no stress, no long ingredient lists, just pure, delicious simplicity.

Now that your pantry is ready, let's dive into the recipes and bring the Mediterranean diet to life, one 5-ingredient dish at a time!

Breakfast Bliss

Greek Yogurt with Chia, Almonds & Berries

Prep: 5 min | **Cook:** 0 min | **Serv:** 2
Ingredients:
- 1 cup Greek yogurt (low-fat)
- 2 tablespoons chia seeds
- ¼ cup mixed berries (strawberries, blueberries, raspberries)
- 1 teaspoon honey
- 1 tablespoon sliced almonds

Instructions:
1. In a bowl, mix Greek yogurt and chia seeds.
2. Divide between two serving bowls.
3. Top with mixed berries, honey, and sliced almonds.
4. Serve immediately or refrigerate for 10 minutes to allow chia seeds to absorb moisture.

Nutritional Information (Per Serving):
Calories: 180 | **Protein:** 14g
Carbs: 15g | **Fat:** 6g | **Fiber:** 4g

Mediterranean Tomato & Feta Scramble

Prep: 5 min | **Cook:** 5 min | **Serv:** 2
Ingredients:
- 4 large eggs
- ½ cup cherry tomatoes, halved
- ¼ cup feta cheese, crumbled
- ½ teaspoon dried oregano
- 1 teaspoon olive oil

Instructions:
1. Whisk the eggs in a bowl and season with dried oregano.
2. Heat olive oil in a non-stick pan over medium heat.
3. Add cherry tomatoes and cook for 2 minutes.
4. Pour in the eggs and scramble gently.
5. Once eggs are fully cooked, remove from heat and sprinkle with feta cheese and serve warm.

Nutritional Information (Per Serving):
Calories: 220 | **Protein:** 16g
Carbs: 4g | **Fat:** 14g | **Fiber:** 1g

Mediterranean Chia Seed Pudding

Prep: 5 min | **Cook:** 0 min | **Serv:** 2
Ingredients:
- 1 cup unsweetened almond milk
- 3 tablespoons chia seeds
- ½ teaspoon vanilla extract
- 1 teaspoon honey
- ¼ teaspoon cinnamon

Instructions:
1. In a jar or bowl, mix the almond milk, chia seeds, vanilla extract, honey, and cinnamon.
2. Stir thoroughly to distribute the chia seeds evenly, then let the mixture sit for 5 minutes before stirring again to prevent clumping.
3. Cover and refrigerate overnight..
4. Stir once more before serving and.

Nutritional Information (Per Serving):
Calories: 150 | **Protein:** 5g
Carbs: 14g | **Fat:** 7g | **Fiber:** 6g

Air-Fried Zucchini & Egg Frittata

Prep: 5 min | **Cook:** 10 min | **Serv:** 2
Ingredients:
- 3 large eggs
- ½ cup zucchini, grated
- ¼ teaspoon black pepper
- ¼ teaspoon dried thyme
- ½ teaspoon olive oil

Instructions:
1. Preheat the air fryer to 350°F (175°C).
2. In a bowl, whisk eggs, black pepper, and dried thyme.
3. Stir in grated zucchini.
4. Lightly grease an air fryer-safe dish with olive oil.
5. Pour the egg mixture into the dish and air-fry for 10 minutes or until set.
6. Let cool slightly before serving.

Nutritional Information (Per Serving):
Calories: 140 | **Protein:** 10g
Carbs: 2g | **Fat:** 10g | **Fiber:** 1g

Mediterranean Almond Flour Pancakes

Prep: 5 min | **Cook:** 10 min | **Serv:** 2

Ingredients:
- ½ cup almond flour
- 2 eggs
- ½ teaspoon baking powder
- ½ teaspoon cinnamon
- 1 teaspoon honey

Instructions:
1. In a bowl, whisk together almond flour, eggs, baking powder, and cinnamon.
2. Heat a non-stick pan over medium heat and lightly grease with olive oil.
3. Pour small amounts of batter into the pan, forming pancakes.
4. Cook for 2-3 minutes on each side until golden brown.
5. Drizzle with honey before serving.

Nutritional Information (Per Serving):
Calories: 180 | **Protein:** 9g
Carbs: 10g | **Fat:** 12g | **Fiber:** 2g

Avocado & Egg Mediterranean Wrap

Prep: 5 min | **Cook:** 5 min | **Serv:** 2

Ingredients:
- 2 whole wheat tortillas
- 1 avocado, mashed
- 2 boiled eggs, sliced
- ¼ teaspoon black pepper
- ½ teaspoon olive oil

Instructions:
1. Spread the mashed avocado evenly onto each tortilla.
2. Arrange the boiled egg slices neatly on top.
3. Sprinkle with black pepper and drizzle with olive oil for added flavor.
4. Roll up the tortilla tightly, ensuring the filling stays secure, and serve immediately.

Nutritional Information (Per Serving):
Calories: 210 | **Protein:** 11g
Carbs: 20g | **Fat:** 10g | **Fiber:** 5g

Mediterranean Chia Pudding with Berries

Prep: 5 min | **Cook:** 0 min | **Serv:** 2

Ingredients:
- 3 tbsp chia seeds
- 1 cup unsweetened almond milk
- ½ tsp vanilla extract
- ½ cup mixed berries (strawberries, blueberries, raspberries)
- 1 tbsp chopped almonds

Instructions:
1. In a bowl or jar, mix the chia seeds, almond milk, and vanilla extract.
2. Stir thoroughly, then let the mixture sit for 5 minutes and stir again.
3. Cover and refrigerate overnight.
4. Before serving, stir again and top with fresh berries and chopped almonds.

Nutritional Information (Per Serving):
Calories: 145 | **Protein:** 4.7g
Carbs: 13.4g | **Fat:** 8.7g | **Fiber:** 8.5g

Cucumber & Labneh Breakfast Bowl

Prep: 5 min | **Cook:** 0 min | **Serv:** 2

Ingredients:
- 1 cup labneh (strained yogurt)
- ½ cup cucumber, diced
- ½ teaspoon za'atar
- ½ teaspoon olive oil
- ¼ teaspoon black pepper

Instructions:
1. Divide the labneh evenly between two serving bowls, smoothing it out with the back of a spoon.
2. Top with diced cucumber, ensuring an even distribution for freshness and crunch.
3. Sprinkle with za'atar and black pepper for a fragrant, slightly earthy flavor.
4. Drizzle with olive oil and serve immediately.

Nutritional Information (Per Serving):
Calories: 160 | **Protein:** 10g
Carbs: 8g | **Fat:** 9g | **Fiber:** 1g

Air-Fried Mediterranean Apple Rings

Prep: 5 min | **Cook:** 8 min | **Serv:** 2

Ingredients:
- 1 large apple, cored and sliced into rings
- ½ teaspoon cinnamon
- 1 teaspoon honey
- ½ teaspoon olive oil
- ¼ teaspoon ground nutmeg

Instructions:
1. Preheat the air fryer to 350°F (175°C).
2. Toss apple rings with cinnamon, nutmeg, and olive oil.
3. Arrange in the air fryer basket and cook for 8 minutes, flipping halfway.
4. Drizzle with honey before serving.

Nutritional Information (Per Serving):
Calories: 140 | **Protein:** 1g
Carbs: 32g | **Fat:** 2g | **Fiber:** 5g

Mediterranean Fig & Almond Smoothie

Prep: 5 min | **Cook:** 0 min | **Serv:** 2

Ingredients:
- 1 cup unsweetened almond milk
- 3 dried figs, chopped
- 1 teaspoon honey
- ¼ teaspoon cinnamon
- 3 ice cubes

Instructions:
1. Add all ingredients to a blender, ensuring the figs are evenly distributed for smooth blending.
2. Blend on high speed for about 30–45 seconds until creamy and smooth. If the mixture is too thick, add a splash of extra almond milk.
3. Pour into glasses and serve immediately.

Nutritional Information (Per Serving):
Calories: 130 | **Protein:** 3g
Carbs: 24g | **Fat:** 4g | **Fiber:** 3g

Cinnamon-Spiced Quinoa Breakfast Bowl

Prep: 5 min | **Cook:** 10 min | **Serv:** 2

Ingredients:
- ½ cup quinoa, rinsed
- 1 cup unsweetened almond milk
- ½ teaspoon cinnamon
- 1 teaspoon honey
- ¼ cup chopped walnuts

Instructions:
1. In a saucepan, bring almond milk to a simmer.
2. Add quinoa and cinnamon, then cook for 10 minutes until fluffy.
3. Stir in honey and divide into two bowls.
4. Top with chopped walnuts and serve warm.

Nutritional Information (Per Serving):
Calories: 180 | **Protein:** 6g
Carbs: 24g | **Fat:** 7g | **Fiber:** 3g

Air-Fried Sweet Potato & Egg Hash

Prep: 5 min | **Cook:** 10 min | **Serv:** 2

Ingredients:
- 1 medium sweet potato, diced
- 2 eggs
- ½ teaspoon paprika
- ½ teaspoon olive oil
- ¼ teaspoon sea salt

Instructions:
1. Preheat air fryer to 375°F (190°C).
2. Toss diced sweet potatoes with olive oil, paprika, and salt.
3. Air-fry for 8 minutes, shaking halfway through.
4. Fry or poach eggs separately and serve on top of the sweet potatoes.

Nutritional Information (Per Serving):
Calories: 200 | **Protein:** 10g
Carbs: 22g | **Fat:** 8g | **Fiber:** 4g

Cottage Cheese & Fig Bowl

Prep: 5 min | **Cook:** 0 min | **Serv:** 2
Ingredients:
- 1 cup cottage cheese
- 2 fresh figs, sliced
- 1 tbsp honey
- 2 tbsp walnuts, chopped
- 1/2 tsp cinnamon

Instructions:
1. Divide the cottage cheese into two bowls.
2. Top with fig slices, honey, and chopped walnuts.
3. Sprinkle with cinnamon and serve immediately.

Nutritional Information (Per Serving):
Calories: 200 | **Protein:** 14g
Carbs: 18g | **Fat:** 6g | **Fiber:** 2.3g

Mediterranean Pear & Ricotta Bowl

Prep: 5 min | **Cook:** 0 min | **Serv:** 2
Ingredients:
- ½ cup ricotta cheese (low-fat)
- 1 small pear, sliced
- 1 teaspoon honey
- ¼ teaspoon cinnamon
- 1 tablespoon chopped almonds

Instructions:
1. Divide ricotta cheese between two bowls.
2. Top with pear slices, honey, and cinnamon.
3. Sprinkle with almonds and serve.

Nutritional Information (Per Serving):
Calories: 180 | **Protein:** 9g
Carbs: 22g | **Fat:** 6g | **Fiber:** 3g

Scrambled Eggs with Sun-Dried Tomatoes & Basil

Prep: 5 min | **Cook:** 5 min | **Serv:** 2

Ingredients:
- 4 eggs
- ¼ cup sun-dried tomatoes, chopped
- ½ teaspoon olive oil
- ¼ teaspoon black pepper
- 2 tablespoons fresh basil, chopped

Instructions:
1. Heat olive oil in a pan over medium heat.
2. Whisk eggs and black pepper, then add to the pan.
3. Stir in sun-dried tomatoes and cook for 3-4 minutes.
4. Sprinkle with fresh basil before serving.

Nutritional Information (Per Serving):
Calories: 220 | **Protein:** 14g
Carbs: 4g | **Fat:** 14g | **Fiber:** 1g

Greek Yogurt & Pistachio Bowl

Prep: 5 min | **Cook:** 0 min | **Serv:** 2

Ingredients:
- 1 cup Greek yogurt (low-fat)
- 1 teaspoon honey
- ¼ teaspoon vanilla extract
- 2 tablespoons pistachios, chopped
- ¼ teaspoon cinnamon

Instructions:
1. In a bowl, mix Greek yogurt with honey and vanilla extract until smooth and well combined.
2. Divide the mixture evenly into two serving bowls.
3. Sprinkle chopped pistachios and cinnamon over the top for added crunch and flavor.
4. Serve immediately.

Nutritional Information (Per Serving):
Calories: 180 | **Protein:** 12g
Carbs: 15g | **Fat:** 7g | **Fiber:** 2g

Baked Ricotta with Honey & Nuts

Prep: 5 min | **Cook:** 15 min | **Serv:** 2

Ingredients:
- 1/2 cup ricotta cheese
- 1 tbsp honey
- 2 tbsp chopped walnuts
- 1/2 tsp vanilla extract
- 1/2 tsp cinnamon

Instructions:
1. Preheat the oven to 375°F (190°C).
2. In a bowl, mix ricotta cheese with vanilla extract and half of the honey.
3. Transfer to a small baking dish and bake for 12-15 minutes until slightly golden on top.
4. Remove from the oven, drizzle with the remaining honey, walnuts and cinnamon.
5. Serve warm with a spoon.

Nutritional Information (Per Serving):
Calories: 230 | **Protein:** 9g
Carbs: 18g | **Fat:** 12g | **Fiber:** 1g

Air-Fried Halloumi & Tomato Bites

Prep: 5 min | **Cook:** 5 min | **Serv:** 2

Ingredients:
- ½ cup halloumi cheese, cubed
- ½ cup cherry tomatoes, halved
- ½ teaspoon olive oil
- ¼ teaspoon oregano
- ¼ teaspoon black pepper

Instructions:
1. Preheat the air fryer to 375°F (190°C).
2. In a bowl, toss the halloumi cubes and cherry tomatoes with olive oil, oregano, and black pepper.
3. Spread the mixture in a single layer in the air fryer basket.
4. Air-fry for 5 minutes, shaking the basket halfway.
5. Serve warm, optionally garnished with fresh basil or a drizzle of balsamic glaze for extra flavor.

Nutritional Information (Per Serving):
Calories: 200 | **Protein:** 12g
Carbs: 6g | **Fat:** 14g | **Fiber:** 1g

Mediterranean Lemon & Honey Porridge

Prep: 5 min | **Cook:** 5 min | **Serv:** 2
Ingredients:
- ½ cup rolled oats
- 1 cup unsweetened almond milk
- ½ teaspoon lemon zest
- 1 teaspoon honey
- ¼ teaspoon cinnamon

Instructions:
1. Bring almond milk to a simmer in a saucepan.
2. Stir in rolled oats and cook for 5 minutes.
3. Remove from heat and stir in honey, lemon zest, and cinnamon.
4. Serve warm.

Nutritional Information (Per Serving):
Calories: 160 | **Protein:** 5g
Carbs: 28g | **Fat:** 4g | **Fiber:** 4g

Dark Chocolate & Walnut Overnight Oats

Prep: 5 min | **Cook:** 0 min | **Serv:** 2
Ingredients:
- ½ cup rolled oats
- 1 cup unsweetened almond milk
- ½ teaspoon cocoa powder
- 1 teaspoon honey
- 2 tablespoons chopped walnuts

Instructions:
1. Mix rolled oats, almond milk, cocoa powder, and honey in a jar.
2. Stir well, cover, and refrigerate overnight.
3. Stir once before serving and top with walnuts.

Nutritional Information (Per Serving):
Calories: 170 | **Protein:** 6g
Carbs: 22g | **Fat:** 7g | **Fiber:** 4g

Satisfying Salads

Cucumber & Dill Yogurt Salad

Prep: 5 min | **Cook:** 0 min | **Serv:** 2

Ingredients:
- 1 large cucumber, thinly sliced
- ½ cup Greek yogurt (low-fat)
- 1 tablespoon fresh dill, chopped
- ½ teaspoon lemon juice
- ¼ teaspoon black pepper

Instructions:
1. In a bowl, mix Greek yogurt, lemon juice, and black pepper.
2. Add sliced cucumber and chopped dill.
3. Toss well to coat the cucumbers evenly.
4. Serve chilled.

Nutritional Information (Per Serving):
Calories: 90 | **Protein:** 6g
Carbs: 10g | **Fat:** 3g | **Fiber:** 2g

Avocado & Cherry Tomato Salad

Prep: 5 min | **Cook:** 0 min | **Serv:** 2

Ingredients:
- 1 ripe avocado, diced
- 1 cup cherry tomatoes, halved
- 1 teaspoon olive oil
- ½ teaspoon balsamic vinegar
- ¼ teaspoon sea salt

Instructions:
1. Combine diced avocado and halved cherry tomatoes in a bowl.
2. Drizzle with olive oil and balsamic vinegar.
3. Sprinkle with sea salt and gently toss.
4. Serve immediately.

Nutritional Information (Per Serving):
Calories: 180 | **Protein:** 3g
Carbs: 12g | **Fat:** 15g | **Fiber:** 6g

Mediterranean Chickpea & Cucumber Salad

Prep: 5 min | **Cook:** 0 min | **Serv:** 2
Ingredients:
- 1 cup canned chickpeas, drained and rinsed
- ½ cucumber, diced
- ½ teaspoon lemon juice
- 1 teaspoon olive oil
- ¼ teaspoon cumin

Instructions:
1. In a bowl, combine chickpeas and diced cucumber.
2. Drizzle with lemon juice and olive oil.
3. Sprinkle with cumin and mix well.
4. Serve fresh or chilled.

Nutritional Information (Per Serving):
Calories: 140 | **Protein:** 6g
Carbs: 18g | **Fat:** 5g | **Fiber:** 5g

Roasted Beet & Walnut Salad

Prep: 5 min | **Cook:** 30 min | **Serv:** 2
Ingredients:
- 2 medium beets, roasted and sliced
- 2 tbsp walnuts, chopped
- 1 tbsp balsamic vinegar
- 1 tbsp olive oil
- 1/4 tsp salt

Instructions:
1. Preheat the oven to 375°F (190°C).
2. Wrap the beets in foil and roast for 30 minutes until tender.
3. Peel and slice the beets, then mix with walnuts.
4. Drizzle with balsamic vinegar and olive oil. Sprinkle with salt and serve.

Nutritional Information (Per Serving):
Calories: 170 | **Protein:** 4g
Carbs: 18g | **Fat:** 10g | **Fiber:** 4.7g

Cabbage & Apple Slaw

Prep: 5 min | **Cook:** 0 min | **Serv: 2**

Ingredients:
- 1 cup shredded cabbage
- 1 small apple, julienned
- 1 tbsp apple cider vinegar
- 1 tbsp olive oil
- 1/2 tsp Dijon mustard

Instructions:
1. In a large bowl, combine the shredded cabbage and julienned apple.
2. In a separate small bowl, whisk together the apple cider vinegar, olive oil, and Dijon mustard.
3. Pour the dressing over the cabbage mixture and toss well.
4. Let it sit for a few minutes to allow the flavors to meld.
5. Serve fresh, optionally garnished with chopped walnuts or a sprinkle of black pepper for added texture and flavor.

Nutritional Information (Per Serving):
Calories: 120 | **Protein:** 2g
Carbs: 14g | **Fat:** 7g | **Fiber:** 2.9g

Roasted Pepper & Feta Salad

Prep: 5 min | **Cook:** 10 min | **Serv: 2**

Ingredients:
- 1 red bell pepper, roasted and sliced
- ¼ cup feta cheese, crumbled
- 1 teaspoon olive oil
- ½ teaspoon red wine vinegar
- ¼ teaspoon black pepper

Instructions:
1. Roast the bell pepper over an open flame or in an oven at 400°F (200°C) for 10 minutes. Let cool, then slice.
2. Arrange sliced bell pepper on a plate.
3. Sprinkle with feta cheese and black pepper.
4. Drizzle with olive oil and red wine vinegar.
5. Serve warm or at room temperature.

Nutritional Information (Per Serving):
Calories: 130 | **Protein:** 5g
Carbs: 10g | **Fat:** 8g | **Fiber:** 2g

Cabbage & Carrot Slaw with Lemon Dressing

Prep: 5 min | **Cook:** 0 min | **Serv:** 2

Ingredients:
- 1 cup shredded cabbage
- ½ cup shredded carrots
- 1 teaspoon olive oil
- ½ teaspoon lemon juice
- ¼ teaspoon ground coriander

Instructions:
1. In a bowl, combine shredded cabbage and carrots.
2. Drizzle with olive oil and lemon juice.
3. Sprinkle with ground coriander and toss well.
4. Serve immediately.

Nutritional Information (Per Serving):
Calories: 90 | **Protein:** 2g
Carbs: 10g | **Fat:** 5g | **Fiber:** 3g

Arugula & Walnut Salad with Lemon Zest

Prep: 5 min | **Cook:** 0 min | **Serv:** 2

Ingredients:
- 2 cups arugula
- ¼ cup walnuts, chopped
- ½ teaspoon lemon zest
- 1 teaspoon olive oil
- ¼ teaspoon sea salt

Instructions:
1. Place arugula in a bowl and top with chopped walnuts.
2. Sprinkle with lemon zest and sea salt.
3. Drizzle with olive oil and toss gently.
4. Serve fresh.

Nutritional Information (Per Serving):
Calories: 140 | **Protein:** 4g
Carbs: 8g | **Fat:** 10g | **Fiber:** 2g

Mediterranean Tomato & Basil Salad

Prep: 5 min | **Cook:** 0 min | **Serv:** 2

Ingredients:
- 1 cup cherry tomatoes, halved
- ¼ cup fresh basil leaves
- 1 teaspoon olive oil
- ½ teaspoon balsamic vinegar
- ¼ teaspoon black pepper

Instructions:
1. In a bowl, combine cherry tomatoes and fresh basil leaves.
2. Drizzle with olive oil and balsamic vinegar.
3. Sprinkle with black pepper and toss gently.
4. Serve fresh.

Nutritional Information (Per Serving):
Calories: 90 | **Protein:** 2g
Carbs: 8g | **Fat:** 6g | **Fiber:** 2g

Zucchini & Mint Salad with Yogurt Dressing

Prep: 5 min | **Cook:** 0 min | **Serv:** 2

Ingredients:
- 1 cup zucchini, spiralized or thinly sliced
- ¼ cup Greek yogurt (low-fat)
- ½ teaspoon lemon juice
- 1 tablespoon fresh mint, chopped
- ¼ teaspoon sea salt

Instructions:
1. In a bowl, mix Greek yogurt, lemon juice, and sea salt.
2. Add spiralized zucchini and chopped mint.
3. Toss well and serve immediately.

Nutritional Information (Per Serving):
Calories: 100 | **Protein:** 5g
Carbs: 10g | **Fat:** 3g | **Fiber:** 2g

Roasted Cauliflower & Chickpea Salad

Prep: 5 min | **Cook:** 15 min | **Serv:** 2
Ingredients:
- 1 cup cauliflower florets
- ½ cup chickpeas, drained and rinsed
- 1 teaspoon olive oil
- ½ teaspoon cumin
- 1 tablespoon lemon juice

Instructions:
1. Preheat oven to 400°F (200°C).
2. Toss cauliflower and chickpeas with olive oil and cumin.
3. Spread on a baking sheet and roast for 15 minutes until golden.
4. Transfer to a bowl, drizzle with lemon juice, and serve.

Nutritional Information (Per Serving):
Calories: 180 | **Protein:** 7g
Carbs: 22g | **Fat:** 6g | **Fiber:** 6g

Avocado & Roasted Tomato Salad

Prep: 5 min | **Cook:** 10 min | **Serv:** 2
Ingredients:
- 1 cup cherry tomatoes, halved
- ½ avocado, diced
- 1 teaspoon olive oil
- ½ teaspoon dried oregano
- 1 tablespoon balsamic vinegar

Instructions:
1. Preheat oven to 375°F (190°C).
2. Toss cherry tomatoes with olive oil and oregano, then roast for 10 minutes.
3. Let cool slightly, then mix with avocado.
4. Drizzle with balsamic vinegar and serve.

Nutritional Information (Per Serving):
Calories: 160 | **Protein:** 3g
Carbs: 14g | **Fat:** 11g | **Fiber:** 5g

Arugula & Roasted Red Pepper Salad

Prep: 5 min | **Cook:** 0 min | **Serv:** 2

Ingredients:
- 2 cups arugula
- ½ cup roasted red peppers, sliced
- 1 tablespoon pine nuts
- 1 teaspoon olive oil
- ½ teaspoon lemon zest

Instructions:
1. Toss arugula with roasted red peppers in a bowl.
2. Sprinkle with pine nuts and lemon zest.
3. Drizzle with olive oil and serve.

Nutritional Information (Per Serving):
Calories: 140 | **Protein:** 3g
Carbs: 8g | **Fat:** 10g | **Fiber:** 3g

Warm Lentil & Carrot Salad

Prep: 5 min | **Cook:** 15 min | **Serv:** 2

Ingredients:
- ½ cup cooked lentils
- ½ cup shredded carrots
- 1 teaspoon olive oil
- ½ teaspoon cumin
- 1 tablespoon lemon juice

Instructions:
1. Heat olive oil in a pan over medium heat.
2. Sauté shredded carrots for 3 minutes, then add cooked lentils.
3. Stir in cumin and cook for 2 more minutes.
4. Remove from heat, drizzle with lemon juice, and serve warm.

Nutritional Information (Per Serving):
Calories: 180 | **Protein:** 10g
Carbs: 22g | **Fat:** 5g | **Fiber:** 8g

Radish & Fennel Crunch Salad

Prep: 5 min | **Cook:** 0 min | **Serv:** 2

Ingredients:
- 1 cup thinly sliced radishes
- ½ cup thinly sliced fennel
- 1 tablespoon lemon juice
- 1 teaspoon olive oil
- ¼ teaspoon sea salt

Instructions:
1. In a bowl, combine radishes and fennel.
2. Drizzle with lemon juice and olive oil.
3. Toss to combine, sprinkle with sea salt, and serve.

Nutritional Information (Per Serving):
Calories: 90 | **Protein:** 2g
Carbs: 10g | **Fat:** 4g | **Fiber:** 3g

Spinach & Roasted Almond Salad

Prep: 5 min | **Cook:** 0 min | **Serv:** 2

Ingredients:
- 2 cups spinach
- 2 tablespoons roasted almonds, chopped
- 1 teaspoon olive oil
- 1 tablespoon balsamic vinegar
- ¼ teaspoon black pepper

Instructions:
1. Toss spinach and roasted almonds in a bowl.
2. Drizzle with olive oil and balsamic vinegar.
3. Sprinkle with black pepper and serve.

Nutritional Information (Per Serving):
Calories: 160 | **Protein:** 5g
Carbs: 10g | **Fat:** 12g | **Fiber:** 3g

Cucumber, Dill & Feta Salad

Prep: 5 min | **Cook:** 0 min | **Serv:** 2

Ingredients:
- 1 cucumber, sliced
- ¼ cup feta cheese, crumbled
- 1 teaspoon olive oil
- ½ teaspoon dried dill
- 1 tablespoon lemon juice

Instructions:
1. In a bowl, combine the sliced cucumber and crumbled feta cheese.
2. Drizzle with olive oil and lemon juice, ensuring even distribution.
3. Sprinkle with dried dill, then toss gently to mix all the flavors.
4. Serve immediately, optionally garnished with freshly ground black pepper or extra feta for added richness.
5. Enjoy as a refreshing side dish or pair with grilled fish or chicken for a light Mediterranean meal.

Nutritional Information (Per Serving):
Calories: 140 | **Protein:** 6g
Carbs: 8g | **Fat:** 9g | **Fiber**: 2g

Roasted Carrot & Chickpea Salad

Prep: 5 min | **Cook:** 20 min | **Serv:** 2

Ingredients:
- 2 medium carrots, sliced
- 1/2 cup canned chickpeas, drained and rinsed
- 2 tbsp olive oil
- 1/2 tsp cumin
- 2 tbsp crumbled feta cheese

Instructions:
1. Preheat the oven to 400°F (200°C).
2. Toss sliced carrots and chickpeas with olive oil and cumin.
3. Spread on a baking sheet and roast for 20 minutes until golden.
4. Transfer to a bowl, sprinkle with crumbled feta, and serve warm or cold.

Nutritional Information (Per Serving):
Calories: 210 | **Protein:** 6g
Carbs: 22g | **Fat:** 11g | **Fiber**: 4.9g

Chickpea & Caper Mediterranean Salad

Prep: 5 min | **Cook:** 0 min | **Serv:** 2

Ingredients:
- ½ cup chickpeas, drained and rinsed
- 1 tablespoon capers
- ½ teaspoon olive oil
- ½ teaspoon dried oregano
- 1 tablespoon lemon juice

Instructions:
1. In a bowl, combine chickpeas and capers.
2. Drizzle with olive oil and lemon juice.
3. Sprinkle with dried oregano, toss, and serve.

Nutritional Information (Per Serving):
Calories: 170 | **Protein**: 7g
Carbs: 18g | **Fat:** 6g | **Fiber:** 5g

Grilled Zucchini & Halloumi Salad

Prep: 5 min | **Cook:** 5 min | **Serv:** 2

Ingredients:
- 1 small zucchini, sliced
- ¼ cup halloumi cheese, cubed
- 1 teaspoon olive oil
- ½ teaspoon black pepper
- ½ teaspoon dried thyme

Instructions:
1. Heat a grill pan over medium heat.
2. Toss zucchini and halloumi with olive oil, thyme, and black pepper.
3. Grill for 5 minutes, turning occasionally.
4. Serve warm.

Nutritional Information (Per Serving):
Calories: 190 | **Protein:** 9g
Carbs: 8g | **Fat:** 14g | **Fiber:** 2g

Snacks & Small Plates

Olive & Caper Tapenade

Prep: 5 min | **Cook:** 0 min | **Serv:** 4

Ingredients:
- ½ cup Kalamata olives, pitted
- 1 tablespoon capers
- ½ teaspoon lemon zest
- 1 teaspoon olive oil
- ½ teaspoon dried oregano

Instructions:
1. Blend all ingredients in a food processor until a chunky paste forms.
2. Serve as a spread on whole wheat crackers or alongside raw veggies.

Nutritional Information (Per Serving):
Calories: 70 | **Protein:** 1g
Carbs: 2g | **Fat:** 6g | **Fiber:** 1g

Baked Feta with Tomatoes

Prep: 5 min | **Cook:** 15 min | **Serv:** 4

Ingredients:
- 4 oz feta cheese
- 1/2 cup cherry tomatoes, halved
- 1 tbsp olive oil
- 1/2 tsp dried thyme
- 1/4 tsp black pepper

Instructions:
1. Preheat the oven to 375°F (190°C).
2. Place feta in a small baking dish and top with cherry tomatoes.
3. Drizzle with olive oil and sprinkle with thyme and pepper.
4. Bake for 15 minutes until soft.

Nutritional Information (Per Serving):
Calories: 130 | **Protein:** 6g
Carbs: 4g | **Fat:** 11g | **Fiber:** 0.3g

Fava Bean & Mint Dip

Prep: 10 min | **Cook:** 0 min | **Serv:** 4

Ingredients:
- 1/2 cup cooked fava beans
- 1 tbsp olive oil
- 1 tbsp lemon juice
- 1 tbsp fresh mint, chopped
- 1/2 tsp cumin

Instructions:
1. In a bowl, mash the cooked fava beans with olive oil, lemon juice, and cumin until smooth but slightly chunky.
2. Stir in the chopped fresh mint, mixing well to evenly distribute the flavors.
3. Serve as a dip with sliced cucumber, bell peppers, or warm pita bread for a refreshing Mediterranean snack.
4. Optionally, drizzle with extra olive oil or garnish with a sprinkle of cumin.

Nutritional Information (Per Serving):
Calories: 100 | **Protein:** 6g
Carbs: 12g | **Fat:** 4g | **Fiber:** 1.3g

Mediterranean Tuna & White Bean Salad

Prep: 5 min | **Cook:** 0 min | **Serv:** 4

Ingredients:
- 1/2 cup canned tuna in olive oil, drained
- 1/2 cup canned white beans, drained
- 1 tbsp lemon juice
- 1 tbsp olive oil
- 1/2 tsp black pepper

Instructions:
1. In a bowl, mix tuna, white beans, olive oil, lemon juice, and black pepper.
2. Stir well and let sit for 5 minutes to absorb flavors.
3. Serve as a light salad on its own, or spread onto whole-grain crackers or toasted bread for a satisfying snack.

Nutritional Information (Per Serving):
Calories: 140 | **Protein:** 12g
Carbs: 10g | **Fat:** 6g | **Fiber:** 1.3g

Stuffed Mini Peppers with Hummus

Prep: 5 min | **Cook:** 0 min | **Serv:** 2

Ingredients:
- 4 mini bell peppers, halved and deseeded
- ½ cup hummus
- ½ teaspoon smoked paprika
- 1 teaspoon olive oil
- ¼ teaspoon sea salt

Instructions:
1. Fill mini bell peppers with hummus.
2. Drizzle with olive oil and sprinkle with smoked paprika and sea salt.
3. Serve fresh.

Nutritional Information (Per Serving):
Calories: 120 | **Protein:** 5g
Carbs: 14g | **Fat:** 6g | **Fiber:** 4g

Zucchini Chips with Garlic & Oregano

Prep: 5 min | **Cook:** 10 min | **Serv:** 2

Ingredients:
- 1 small zucchini, thinly sliced
- 1 teaspoon olive oil
- ¼ teaspoon garlic powder
- ¼ teaspoon dried oregano
- ¼ teaspoon sea salt

Instructions:
1. Preheat oven to 375°F (190°C).
2. Toss zucchini slices with olive oil, garlic powder, oregano, and sea salt.
3. Arrange on a baking sheet and bake for 10 minutes until crispy.
4. Let cool before serving.

Nutritional Information (Per Serving):
Calories: 90 | **Protein:** 2g
Carbs: 10g | **Fat:** 5g | **Fiber:** 2g

Air-Fried Eggplant Chips with Lemon Zest

Prep: 5 min | **Cook:** 10 min | **Serv:** 2

Ingredients:
- 1 small eggplant, thinly sliced
- 1 teaspoon olive oil
- ½ teaspoon lemon zest
- ¼ teaspoon black pepper
- ¼ teaspoon sea salt

Instructions:
1. Preheat air fryer to 375°F (190°C).
2. Toss eggplant slices with olive oil, lemon zest, black pepper, and sea salt.
3. Air fry for 10 minutes, flipping halfway through.
4. Serve immediately.

Nutritional Information (Per Serving):
Calories: 80 | **Protein:** 1g
Carbs: 10g | **Fat:** 4g | **Fiber:** 3g

Marinated Artichoke & Olive Skewers

Prep: 5 min | **Cook:** 0 min | **Serv:** 2

Ingredients:
- 4 marinated artichoke hearts, halved
- 8 Kalamata olives
- 1 teaspoon olive oil
- ½ teaspoon lemon juice
- ¼ teaspoon black pepper

Instructions:
1. Thread artichoke hearts and olives onto skewers.
2. Drizzle with olive oil and lemon juice.
3. Sprinkle with black pepper and serve.

Nutritional Information (Per Serving):
Calories: 90 | **Protein:** 2g
Carbs: 6g | **Fat:** 7g | **Fiber:** 3g

Roasted Red Pepper & Walnut Dip

Prep: 5 min | **Cook:** 0 min | **Serv:** 4

Ingredients:
- ½ cup roasted red peppers
- ¼ cup walnuts
- 1 teaspoon olive oil
- ¼ teaspoon cumin
- ¼ teaspoon sea salt

Instructions:
1. In a food processor or blender, combine the roasted red peppers, walnuts, olive oil, cumin, and sea salt.
2. Blend until smooth, scraping down the sides as needed to ensure even consistency.
3. Serve as a dip with whole wheat crackers, fresh veggies, or warm pita bread. Optionally, drizzle with extra olive oil or garnish with chopped parsley.

Nutritional Information (Per Serving):
Calories: 90 | **Protein:** 2g
Carbs: 6g | **Fat:** 7g | **Fiber:** 2g

Grilled Mushroom & Thyme Bites

Prep: 5 min | **Cook:** 10 min | **Serv:** 2

Ingredients:
- 6 button mushrooms, halved
- 1 teaspoon olive oil
- ½ teaspoon dried thyme
- ¼ teaspoon garlic powder
- ¼ teaspoon sea salt

Instructions:
1. Preheat grill or pan to medium heat.
2. In a bowl, toss the halved mushrooms with olive oil, thyme, garlic powder, and sea salt until evenly coated.
3. Place mushrooms on the grill, cut side down, and cook for about 5 minutes per side.
4. Serve warm, optionally garnished with fresh thyme or a drizzle of balsamic glaze for added flavor.

Nutritional Information (Per Serving):
Calories: 80 | **Protein:** 3g
Carbs: 6g | **Fat:** 5g | **Fiber:** 2g

Lemon & Herb Marinated Feta Cubes

Prep: 5 min | **Cook:** 0 min | **Serv:** 2
Ingredients:
- ½ cup feta cheese, cut into cubes
- 1 teaspoon olive oil
- ½ teaspoon lemon juice
- ½ teaspoon dried oregano
- ¼ teaspoon black pepper

Instructions:
1. In a bowl, toss the feta cubes with olive oil, lemon juice, oregano, and black pepper until evenly coated.
2. Let marinate for 5 minutes.
3. Serve as a standalone appetizer, or pair with olives, toasted bread, or a fresh Mediterranean salad for extra flavor.

Nutritional Information (Per Serving):
Calories: 100 | **Protein:** 5g
Carbs: 2g | **Fat:** 8g | **Fiber:** 0g

Spinach & Cheese Bites

Prep: 10 min | **Cook:** 15 min | **Serv:** 4
Ingredients:
- 1 cup fresh spinach, chopped
- 1/2 cup feta cheese, crumbled
- 1 egg, beaten
- 1 tbsp whole wheat flour
- 1/2 tsp dried oregano

Instructions:
1. Preheat oven to 375°F (190°C).
2. In a bowl, mix chopped spinach, feta cheese, egg, flour, and oregano until well combined.
3. Form small patties and place on a baking sheet lined with parchment paper.
4. Bake for 15 minutes until golden brown.
5. Let cool slightly and serve warm.

Nutritional Information (Per Serving):
Calories: 130 | **Protein:** 7g
Carbs: 6g | **Fat:** 9g | **Fiber:** 0.5g

Stuffed Dates with Almond Butter

Prep: 5 min | **Cook:** 0 min | **Serv:** 4

Ingredients:
- 8 Medjool dates, pitted
- 4 teaspoons almond butter
- 1 teaspoon honey
- 1 tablespoon crushed pistachios
- ¼ teaspoon cinnamon

Instructions:
1. Slice dates lengthwise and remove pits.
2. Fill each date with ½ teaspoon of almond butter.
3. Drizzle with honey and sprinkle with crushed pistachios and cinnamon.
4. Serve immediately.

Nutritional Information (Per Serving - 2 dates):
Calories: 160 | **Protein:** 3g
Carbs: 26g | **Fat:** 6g | **Fiber:** 3g

Air-Fried Zucchini Parmesan Bites

Prep: 5 min | **Cook:** 8 min | **Serv:** 2

Ingredients:
- 1 medium zucchini, sliced into rounds
- 2 tablespoons grated Parmesan cheese
- 1 teaspoon olive oil
- ½ teaspoon oregano
- ¼ teaspoon garlic powder

Instructions:
1. Preheat air fryer to 375°F (190°C).
2. Toss zucchini slices with olive oil, oregano, and garlic powder.
3. Arrange in air fryer basket and sprinkle with Parmesan cheese.
4. Air-fry for 8 minutes until crispy and golden.

Nutritional Information (Per Serving):
Calories: 120 | **Protein:** 6g
Carbs: 7g | **Fat:** 8g | **Fiber:** 2g

Marinated Cherry Tomatoes with Basil

Prep: 5 min | **Cook:** 0 min | **Serv:** 2

Ingredients:
- 1 cup cherry tomatoes, halved
- 1 teaspoon olive oil
- 1 teaspoon balsamic vinegar
- ¼ teaspoon black pepper
- 2 tablespoons fresh basil, chopped

Instructions:
1. Toss cherry tomatoes with olive oil, balsamic vinegar, and black pepper.
2. Stir in fresh basil and let marinate for 5 minutes
3. Serve as a refreshing side dish, a topping for grilled meats, or spooned over toasted bread for a simple bruschetta.

Nutritional Information (Per Serving):
Calories: 70 | **Protein:** 1g
Carbs: 5g | **Fat:** 5g | **Fiber:** 2g

Stuffed Grape Leaves with Lemon & Herbs

Prep: 15 min | **Cook:** 20 min | **Serv:** 4

Ingredients:
- 8 grape leaves, rinsed
- 1/2 cup cooked quinoa
- 1 tbsp olive oil
- 1 tbsp lemon juice
- 1/2 tsp dried mint

Instructions:
1. In a bowl, mix cooked quinoa, olive oil, lemon juice, and dried mint.
2. Lay out grape leaves and place a small amount of the filling in each.
3. Roll tightly, tucking in the sides.
4. Place in a steamer and steam for 20 minutes.
5. Serve warm or chilled.

Nutritional Information (Per Serving):
Calories: 90 | **Protein:** 3g
Carbs: 10g | **Fat:** 4g | **Fiber:** 0.9g

Crispy Zucchini & Parmesan Bites

Prep: 10 min | **Cook:** 15 min | **Serv:** 4

Ingredients:
- 1 medium zucchini, grated
- 2 tbsp grated Parmesan cheese
- 1 egg, beaten
- 1 tbsp whole wheat flour
- 1/2 tsp garlic powder

Instructions:
1. Preheat oven to 375°F (190°C).
2. In a bowl, mix grated zucchini, Parmesan, egg, flour, and garlic powder.
3. Form small bites and place on a parchment-lined baking sheet.
4. Bake for 15 minutes until golden and crispy.
5. Serve warm with Greek yogurt dip.

Nutritional Information (Per Serving):
Calories: 110 | **Protein:** 6g
Carbs: 8g | **Fat:** 5g | **Fiber:** 0.7g

Eggplant & Chickpea Patties

Prep: 10 min | **Cook:** 15 min | **Serv:** 4

Ingredients:
- 1/2 cup cooked chickpeas, mashed
- 1/2 cup roasted eggplant, mashed
- 1 tbsp whole wheat flour
- 1 tbsp olive oil
- 1/2 tsp cumin

Instructions:
1. In a bowl, mix mashed chickpeas, roasted eggplant, flour, olive oil, and cumin until combined.
2. Form small patties and place on a parchment-lined baking sheet.
3. Bake at 375°F (190°C) for 15 minutes, flipping halfway through.
4. Serve warm with yogurt dip or lemon wedges.

Nutritional Information (Per Serving):
Calories: 130 | **Protein:** 5g
Carbs: 14g | **Fat:** 6g | **Fiber:** 2.5g

Zesty Carrot & Cumin Dip

Prep: 10 min | **Cook:** 10 min | **Serv:** 4
Ingredients:
- 1 cup carrots, boiled and mashed
- 1 tbsp olive oil
- 1 tbsp lemon juice
- 1/2 tsp cumin
- 1/2 tsp smoked paprika

Instructions:
1. In a bowl, mix mashed carrots with olive oil, lemon juice, cumin, and smoked paprika.
2. Stir well until smooth.
3. Serve chilled with cucumber sticks or whole-grain crackers.

Nutritional Information (Per Serving):
Calories: 90 | **Protein:** 1g
Carbs: 9g | **Fat:** 5g | **Fiber:** 1g

Air-Fried Stuffed Mushrooms

Prep: 5 min | **Cook:** 10 min | **Serv:** 2
Ingredients:
- 6 large mushrooms, stems removed
- ¼ cup feta cheese, crumbled
- 1 teaspoon olive oil
- ¼ teaspoon black pepper
- ½ teaspoon oregano

Instructions:
1. Preheat air fryer to 375°F (190°C).
2. Stuff mushrooms with feta cheese and drizzle with olive oil.
3. Sprinkle with black pepper and oregano.
4. Air-fry for 10 minutes until golden and tender.

Nutritional Information (Per Serving):
Calories: 130 | **Protein:** 6g
Carbs: 5g | **Fat:** 10g | **Fiber:** 2g

Roasted Red Pepper & Garlic Dip

Prep: 5 min | **Cook:** 10 min | **Serv:** 4

Ingredients:
- 1 large red bell pepper
- 1 teaspoon olive oil
- 1 garlic clove, minced
- ¼ teaspoon sea salt
- ¼ teaspoon smoked paprika

Instructions:
1. Roast red bell pepper at 400°F (200°C) for 10 minutes.
2. Let cool, then blend with olive oil, garlic, sea salt, and smoked paprika.
3. Serve with whole wheat crackers or cucumber slices.

Nutritional Information (Per Serving):
Calories: 80 | **Protein:** 2g
Carbs: 6g | **Fat:** 5g | **Fiber:** 2g

Zucchini Fritters with Dill

Prep: 10 min | **Cook:** 10 min | **Serv:** 4

Ingredients:
- 1 medium zucchini, grated
- 1 egg, beaten
- 2 tbsp chickpea flour
- 1 tbsp fresh dill, chopped
- 1 tbsp olive oil

Instructions:
1. Squeeze excess water from grated zucchini.
2. In a bowl, mix zucchini, egg, chickpea flour, and dill.
3. Heat olive oil in a pan over medium heat.
4. Form small fritters and fry for 3-4 minutes per side until golden brown.

Nutritional Information (Per Serving):
Calories: 120 | **Protein:** 5g
Carbs: 10g | **Fat:** 7g | **Fiber:** 0.95g

Quick & Easy Main Dishes

Lemon Garlic Shrimp with Zucchini Noodles

Prep: 5 min | **Cook:** 10 min | **Serv:** 2

Ingredients:
- 1 cup shrimp, peeled and deveined
- 2 small zucchinis, spiralized
- 1 teaspoon olive oil
- ½ teaspoon garlic powder
- ½ teaspoon lemon zest

Instructions:
1. Heat olive oil in a skillet over medium heat.
2. Add shrimp and season with garlic powder. Cook for 3-4 minutes until pink.
3. Add spiralized zucchini and lemon zest. Toss and cook for 2 more minutes.
4. Serve immediately.

Nutritional Information (Per Serving):
Calories: 180 | **Protein:** 24g
Carbs: 8g | **Fat:** 6g | **Fiber:** 2g

Garlic & Herb Turkey Meatballs

Prep: 5 min | **Cook:** 15 min | **Serv:** 4

Ingredients:
- 1/2 lb ground turkey
- 1 tbsp fresh parsley, chopped
- 1 tbsp olive oil
- 1/2 tsp garlic powder
- 1/2 tsp black pepper

Instructions:
1. Preheat oven to 375°F (190°C).
2. Mix ground turkey with parsley, garlic powder, and black pepper.
3. Form small meatballs (about 1 inch in diameter) and arrange them evenly on the baking sheet.
4. Drizzle with olive oil and bake for 15 minutes.
5. Serve warm as a main dish, with a side of roasted vegetables.

Nutritional Information (Per Serving):
Calories: 190 | **Protein:** 22g
Carbs: 1g | **Fat:** 10g | **Fiber:** 0.1g

Mediterranean Lentil & Spinach Stir-Fry

Prep: 5 min | **Cook:** 10 min | **Serv:** 2

Ingredients:
- 1 cup cooked lentils
- 1 cup fresh spinach
- 1 teaspoon olive oil
- ½ teaspoon cumin
- ¼ teaspoon sea salt

Instructions:
1. Heat olive oil in a pan over medium heat.
2. Add the cooked lentils, fresh spinach, cumin, and sea salt, stirring well to coat the ingredients with the seasoning
3. Stir-fry for about 5 minutes, or until the spinach is wilted and the lentils are heated through..
4. Serve warm.

Nutritional Information (Per Serving):
Calories: 190 | **Protein:** 12g
Carbs: 24g | **Fat:** 6g | **Fiber:** 8g

One-Pan Mediterranean Turkey Skillet

Prep: 5 min | **Cook:** 15 min | **Serv:** 2

Ingredients:
- 1 cup ground turkey (lean)
- ½ cup cherry tomatoes, halved
- 1 teaspoon olive oil
- ½ teaspoon dried oregano
- ¼ teaspoon garlic powder

Instructions:
1. Heat olive oil in a skillet over medium heat.
2. Add ground turkey and cook for 5 minutes, breaking it up.
3. Stir in cherry tomatoes, oregano, and garlic powder. Cook for another 10 minutes.
4. Serve warm.

Nutritional Information (Per Serving):
Calories: 220 | **Protein:** 28g
Carbs: 6g | **Fat:** 9g | **Fiber:** 2g

Mediterranean Stuffed Bell Peppers

Prep: 5 min | **Cook:** 15 min | **Serv:** 2
Ingredients:
- 2 bell peppers, halved and deseeded
- 1 cup cooked quinoa
- ¼ cup feta cheese, crumbled
- 1 teaspoon olive oil
- ¼ teaspoon dried thyme

Instructions:
1. Preheat oven to 375°F (190°C).
2. Mix cooked quinoa, feta cheese, olive oil, and thyme.
3. Stuff the bell peppers with the mixture.
4. Bake for 15 minutes and serve warm.

Nutritional Information (Per Serving):
Calories: 200 | **Protein:** 9g
Carbs: 28g | **Fat:** 6g | **Fiber:** 5g

Mediterranean Baked Cod with Lemon & Herbs

Prep: 5 min | **Cook:** 15 min | **Serv:** 2
Ingredients:
- 2 small cod fillets
- 1 teaspoon olive oil
- ½ teaspoon dried oregano
- ½ teaspoon lemon zest
- ¼ teaspoon sea salt

Instructions:
1. Preheat oven to 375°F (190°C).
2. Rub cod fillets with olive oil, oregano, lemon zest, and sea salt.
3. Place the fillets in the prepared baking dish and bake for 15 minutes, or until the fish flakes easily with a fork.
4. Serve hot.

Nutritional Information (Per Serving):
Calories: 180 | **Protein:** 28g
Carbs: 1g | **Fat:** 6g | **Fiber:** 0g

Chickpea & Spinach Stir-Fry

Prep: 5 min | **Cook:** 10 min | **Serv:** 2

Ingredients:
- 1 cup canned chickpeas, drained and rinsed
- 1 cup fresh spinach
- 1 teaspoon olive oil
- ½ teaspoon cumin
- ¼ teaspoon black pepper

Instructions:
1. Heat olive oil in a skillet over medium heat.
2. Add chickpeas and cumin, stirring for 5 minutes.
3. Add spinach and black pepper, cooking until wilted.
4. Serve immediately.

Nutritional Information (Per Serving):
Calories: 190 | **Protein:** 9g
Carbs: 24g | **Fat:** 6g | **Fiber:** 6g

Garlic & Herb Grilled Chicken Breasts

Prep: 5 min | **Cook:** 15 min | **Serv:** 2

Ingredients:
- 2 small chicken breasts
- 1 teaspoon olive oil
- ½ teaspoon garlic powder
- ½ teaspoon dried thyme
- ¼ teaspoon sea salt

Instructions:
1. Preheat grill to medium heat.
2. Rub chicken breasts with olive oil, garlic powder, thyme, and sea salt.
3. Grill for 15 minutes per side until cooked through.
4. Serve warm.

Nutritional Information (Per Serving):
Calories: 220 | **Protein:** 28g
Carbs: 1g | **Fat:** 9g | **Fiber:** 0g

Roasted Eggplant & Tomato Stew

Prep: 5 min | **Cook:** 15 min | **Serv:** 2
Ingredients:
- 1 small eggplant, sliced
- ½ cup cherry tomatoes, halved
- 1 teaspoon olive oil
- ½ teaspoon dried basil
- ¼ teaspoon black pepper

Instructions:
1. Heat olive oil in a pot over medium heat.
2. Add eggplant, tomatoes, basil, and black pepper.
3. Cook for 15 minutes, stirring occasionally.
4. Serve warm, optionally garnished with fresh basil or a drizzle of extra olive oil for added depth of flavor.

Nutritional Information (Per Serving):
Calories: 140 | **Protein:** 3g
Carbs: 18g | **Fat:** 7g | **Fiber:** 5g

Garlic Lemon Shrimp with Zucchini Noodles

Prep: 5 min | **Cook:** 15 min | **Serv:** 2
Ingredients:
- 8 large shrimp, peeled and deveined
- 1 medium zucchini, spiralized
- 1 teaspoon olive oil
- 1 garlic clove, minced
- 1 tablespoon lemon juice

Instructions:
1. Heat olive oil in a pan over medium heat.
2. Add minced garlic and sauté for 30 seconds.
3. Add shrimp and cook for 5 minutes on each side.
4. Stir in zucchini noodles and lemon juice, cooking for 5 more minutes.
5. Serve immediately.

Nutritional Information (Per Serving):
Calories: 180 | **Protein:** 22g
Carbs: 6g | **Fat:** 7g | **Fiber:** 2g

Greek-Style Baked Chicken Thighs

Prep: 5 min | **Cook:** 20 min | **Serv:** 2

Ingredients:
- 2 boneless, skinless chicken thighs
- 1 teaspoon olive oil
- ½ teaspoon oregano
- ½ teaspoon garlic powder
- 1 tablespoon lemon juice

Instructions:
1. Preheat oven to 375°F (190°C).
2. Rub chicken thighs with olive oil, oregano, and garlic powder.
3. Place on a baking sheet and bake for 20 minutes.
4. Drizzle with lemon juice before serving.

Nutritional Information (Per Serving):
Calories: 210 | **Protein:** 25g
Carbs: 2g | **Fat:** 12g | **Fiber:** 0g

Mediterranean Lentil & Spinach Stir-Fry

Prep: 5 min | **Cook:** 10 min | **Serv:** 2

Ingredients:
- ½ cup cooked lentils
- 2 cups fresh spinach
- 1 teaspoon olive oil
- ½ teaspoon cumin
- 1 garlic clove, minced

Instructions:
1. Heat olive oil in a pan over medium heat.
2. Add garlic and sauté for 30 seconds.
3. Stir in lentils and cumin, cooking for 3 minutes.
4. Add spinach and cook until wilted (about 2 minutes).
5. Serve warm.

Nutritional Information (Per Serving):
Calories: 190 | **Protein:** 12g
Carbs: 22g | **Fat:** 6g | **Fiber:** 8g

Grilled Salmon with Olive Tapenade

Prep: 5 min | **Cook:** 10 min | **Serv:** 2

Ingredients:
- 2 salmon fillets (4 oz each)
- 1 teaspoon olive oil
- 2 tablespoons chopped olives
- ½ teaspoon dried oregano
- 1 tablespoon lemon juice

Instructions:
1. Preheat grill to medium-high heat.
2. Rub salmon fillets with olive oil and oregano.
3. Grill for 4-5 minutes on each side.
4. Top with chopped olives and lemon juice before serving.

Nutritional Information (Per Serving):
Calories: 230 | **Protein:** 25g
Carbs: 3g | **Fat:** 14g | **Fiber:** 1g

Balsamic Glazed Chicken & Mushrooms

Prep: 5 min | **Cook:** 20 min | **Serv:** 4

Ingredients:
- 2 boneless, skinless chicken breasts
- 1 cup mushrooms, sliced
- 1 tbsp balsamic vinegar
- 1 tbsp olive oil
- 1/2 tsp black pepper

Instructions:
1. Heat olive oil in a skillet over medium heat.
2. Cook chicken breasts for 10 minutes per side.
3. Add mushrooms, balsamic vinegar, and black pepper.
4. Cook for another 5 minutes until tender.

Nutritional Information (Per Serving):
Calories: 210 | **Protein:** 30g
Carbs: 5g | **Fat:** 7g | **Fiber:** 0.2g

Spiced Turkey & Zucchini Skillet

Prep: 5 min | **Cook:** 15 min | **Serv:** 4

Ingredients:
- 1/2 lb ground turkey
- 1 medium zucchini, diced
- 1 tbsp olive oil
- 1/2 tsp cumin
- 1/2 tsp dried oregano

Instructions:
1. Heat olive oil in a skillet over medium heat.
2. Add ground turkey and cook for 5 minutes, breaking it apart.
3. Stir in diced zucchini, cumin, and oregano. Cook for another 8-10 minutes until the turkey is fully cooked.
4. Serve warm as a protein-packed main dish.

Nutritional Information (Per Serving):
Calories: 190 | **Protein:** 22g
Carbs: 4g | **Fat:** 10g | **Fiber:** 0.6g

Mediterranean Duck with Cherry Sauce

Prep: 5 min | **Cook:** 15 min | **Serv:** 2

Ingredients:
- 2 skinless duck breasts
- 1/2 cup fresh or frozen cherries, pitted
- 1 tbsp balsamic vinegar
- 1 tbsp honey
- 1/2 tsp dried thyme

Instructions:
1. Preheat a pan over medium heat. Lightly coat with a few drops of olive oil.
2. Cook the duck breasts for 4-5 minutes per side.
3. In the same pan, add cherries, balsamic vinegar, honey, and thyme. Simmer for 5 minutes.
4. Slice the duck, drizzle with cherry sauce, and serve with grilled vegetables or a light salad.

Nutritional Information (Per Serving):
Calories: 260 | **Protein:** 30g
Carbs: 12g | **Fat:** 8g | **Fiber:** 0.9g

Zucchini & Chickpea Stew

Prep: 5 min | **Cook:** 20 min | **Serv:** 4
Ingredients:
- 1 medium zucchini, diced
- 1/2 cup canned chickpeas, drained
- 1 tbsp olive oil
- 1/2 tsp smoked paprika
- 1/2 cup crushed tomatoes

Instructions:
1. Heat olive oil in a pot over medium heat.
2. Add zucchini and sauté for 5 minutes.
3. Stir in chickpeas, smoked paprika, and crushed tomatoes.
4. Simmer for 15 minutes until the flavors meld together.

Nutritional Information (Per Serving):
Calories: 170 | **Protein:** 6g
Carbs: 20g | **Fat:** 7g | **Fiber:** 2.6g

Roasted Eggplant & Tahini Bowl

Prep: 5 min | **Cook:** 20 min | **Serv:** 4
Ingredients:
- 1 medium eggplant, diced
- 1 tbsp olive oil
- 1 tbsp tahini
- 1 tbsp lemon juice
- 1/2 tsp cumin

Instructions:
1. Preheat oven to 400°F (200°C).
2. Toss diced eggplant with olive oil and roast for 20 minutes.
3. In a bowl, mix tahini, lemon juice, and cumin.
4. Drizzle sauce over roasted eggplant before serving.

Nutritional Information (Per Serving):
Calories: 180 | **Protein:** 4g
Carbs: 12g | **Fat:** 10g | **Fiber:** 3.3g

Stuffed Peppers with Tuna & Olives

Prep: 5 min | **Cook:** 15 min | **Serv:** 4

Ingredients:
- 2 large bell peppers, halved and seeded
- 1/2 cup canned tuna in olive oil, drained
- 1/4 cup Kalamata olives, chopped
- 1 tbsp lemon juice
- 1 tbsp fresh parsley, chopped

Instructions:
1. Preheat oven to 375°F (190°C).
2. In a bowl, mix tuna, olives, lemon juice, and parsley.
3. Stuff the bell pepper halves with the mixture.
4. Bake for 15 minutes until the peppers soften.
5. Serve warm with a drizzle of extra olive oil if desired.

Nutritional Information (Per Serving):
Calories: 180 | **Protein:** 18g
Carbs: 7g | **Fat:** 9g | **Fiber:** 2g

Chickpea & Egg Skillet

Prep: 5 min | **Cook:** 15 min | **Serv:** 4

Ingredients:
- 1/2 cup canned chickpeas, drained
- 2 eggs
- 1/2 cup cherry tomatoes, halved
- 1 tbsp olive oil
- 1/2 tsp smoked paprika

Instructions:
1. Heat olive oil in a skillet over medium heat.
2. Add chickpeas and cherry tomatoes, sauté for 5 minutes.
3. Sprinkle with smoked paprika and crack eggs over the mixture.
4. Cover and cook for another 5 minutes until the eggs are set.

Nutritional Information (Per Serving):
Calories: 190 | **Protein:** 10g
Carbs: 16g | **Fat:** 9g | **Fiber:** 1.9g

Flavorful Side Dishes

Roasted Garlic Green Beans

Prep: 5 min | **Cook:** 10 min | **Serv:** 2

Ingredients:
- 2 cups green beans, trimmed
- 1 teaspoon olive oil
- ½ teaspoon garlic powder
- ¼ teaspoon black pepper
- ¼ teaspoon sea salt

Instructions:
1. Preheat oven to 375°F (190°C).
2. Toss green beans with olive oil, garlic powder, black pepper, and salt.
3. Spread on a baking sheet and roast for 10 minutes.
4. Serve warm.

Nutritional Information (Per Serving):
Calories: 80 | **Protein:** 3g
Carbs: 10g | **Fat:** 4g | **Fiber:** 4g

Lemon & Thyme Roasted Carrots

Prep: 5 min | **Cook:** 15 min | **Serv:** 2

Ingredients:
- 2 medium carrots, sliced
- 1 teaspoon olive oil
- ½ teaspoon lemon zest
- ½ teaspoon dried thyme
- ¼ teaspoon sea salt

Instructions:
1. Preheat oven to 375°F (190°C).
2. Toss sliced carrots with olive oil, lemon zest, thyme, and sea salt.
3. Spread on a baking sheet and roast for 15 minutes.
4. Serve warm.

Nutritional Information (Per Serving):
Calories: 90 | **Protein:** 2g
Carbs: 14g | **Fat:** 4g | **Fiber:** 3g

Sautéed Zucchini with Garlic & Oregano

Prep: 5 min | **Cook:** 10 min | **Serv:** 2

Ingredients:
- 1 medium zucchini, sliced
- 1 teaspoon olive oil
- ½ teaspoon garlic powder
- ½ teaspoon dried oregano
- ¼ teaspoon sea salt

Instructions:
1. Heat olive oil in a skillet over medium heat.
2. Add zucchini, garlic powder, oregano, and sea salt.
3. Sauté for 10 minutes until tender.
4. Serve warm.

Nutritional Information (Per Serving):
Calories: 70 | **Protein:** 2g
Carbs: 9g | **Fat:** 4g | **Fiber:** 2g

Mediterranean Roasted Bell Peppers

Prep: 5 min | **Cook:** 15 min | **Serv:** 2

Ingredients:
- 1 red bell pepper, sliced
- 1 yellow bell pepper, sliced
- 1 teaspoon olive oil
- ½ teaspoon balsamic vinegar
- ¼ teaspoon black pepper

Instructions:
1. Preheat oven to 375°F (190°C).
2. Toss bell peppers with olive oil, balsamic vinegar, and black pepper.
3. Spread on a baking sheet and roast for 15 minutes.
4. Serve warm or at room temperature.

Nutritional Information (Per Serving):
Calories: 80 | **Protein:** 1g
Carbs: 12g | **Fat:** 4g | **Fiber:** 3g

Ingredient Mediterranean Quinoa & Parsley Salad

Prep: 5 min | **Cook:** 15 min | **Serv:** 4

Ingredients:
- 1/2 cup quinoa, cooked
- 1 tbsp olive oil
- 1 tbsp lemon juice
- 2 tbsp fresh parsley, chopped
- 1/4 tsp sea salt

Instructions:
1. In a bowl, mix cooked quinoa, olive oil, lemon juice, and parsley.
2. Sprinkle with sea salt and mix well.

Nutritional Information (Per Serving):
Calories: 140 | **Protein:** 4g
Carbs: 18g | **Fat:** 5g | **Fiber:** 0.7g

Cumin-Spiced Roasted Cauliflower

Prep: 5 min | **Cook:** 15 min | **Serv:** 2

Ingredients:
- 2 cups cauliflower florets
- 1 teaspoon olive oil
- ½ teaspoon cumin
- ¼ teaspoon paprika
- ¼ teaspoon sea salt

Instructions:
1. Preheat oven to 375°F (190°C).
2. Toss cauliflower with olive oil, cumin, paprika, and sea salt.
3. Spread on a baking sheet and roast for 15 minutes.
4. Serve warm.

Nutritional Information (Per Serving):
Calories: 90 | **Protein:** 3g
Carbs: 10g | **Fat:** 5g | **Fiber:** 4g

Roasted Cherry Tomatoes with Basil

Prep: 5 min | **Cook:** 10 min | **Serv:** 2

Ingredients:
- 1 cup cherry tomatoes
- 1 teaspoon olive oil
- ½ teaspoon dried basil
- ¼ teaspoon black pepper
- ¼ teaspoon sea salt

Instructions:
1. Preheat oven to 375°F (190°C).
2. Toss cherry tomatoes with olive oil, basil, black pepper, and sea salt.
3. Spread on a baking sheet and roast for 10 minutes.
4. Serve warm or as a topping for other dishes.

Nutritional Information (Per Serving):
Calories: 70 | **Protein:** 2g
Carbs: 9g | **Fat:** 4g | **Fiber:** 2g

Lemon & Garlic Roasted Brussels Sprouts

Prep: 5 min | **Cook:** 15 min | **Serv:** 2

Ingredients:
- 1 cup Brussels sprouts, halved
- 1 teaspoon olive oil
- ½ teaspoon lemon juice
- ¼ teaspoon garlic powder
- ¼ teaspoon sea salt

Instructions:
1. Preheat oven to 375°F (190°C).
2. Toss Brussels sprouts with olive oil, lemon juice, garlic powder, and sea salt.
3. Spread on a baking sheet and roast for 15 minutes.
4. Serve warm.

Nutritional Information (Per Serving):
Calories: 90 | **Protein:** 4g
Carbs: 12g | **Fat:** 5g | **Fiber:** 4g

Roasted Brussels Sprouts with Balsamic Glaze

Prep: 5 min | **Cook:** 20 min | **Serv:** 4

Ingredients:
- 2 cups Brussels sprouts, halved
- 1 tbsp olive oil
- 1 tbsp balsamic vinegar
- 1/4 tsp black pepper
- 1/4 tsp sea salt

Instructions:
1. Preheat oven to 400°F (200°C).
2. Toss Brussels sprouts with olive oil, salt, and black pepper.
3. Roast for 20 minutes, then drizzle with balsamic vinegar before serving.

Nutritional Information (Per Serving):
Calories: 110 | **Protein:** 4g
Carbs: 12g | **Fat:** 5g | **Fiber:** 1.7g

Sweet Potatoes with Paprika

Prep: 5 min | **Cook:** 25 min | **Serv:** 4

Ingredients:
- 2 medium sweet potatoes, diced
- 1 tbsp olive oil
- 1/2 tsp smoked paprika
- 1/4 tsp sea salt
- 1 tbsp chopped fresh parsley

Instructions:
1. Preheat oven to 400°F (200°C).
2. Toss sweet potatoes with olive oil, smoked paprika, and salt.
3. Roast for 25 minutes until golden.
4. Garnish with fresh parsley before serving.

Nutritional Information (Per Serving):
Calories: 160 | **Protein:** 2g
Carbs: 25g | **Fat:** 6g | **Fiber:** 2.1g

Roasted Fennel with Lemon & Olive Oil

Prep: 5 min | **Cook:** 25 min | **Serv:** 4
Ingredients:
- 1 large fennel bulb, sliced
- 1 tbsp olive oil
- 1 tbsp lemon juice
- 1/4 tsp sea salt
- 1/2 tsp dried thyme

Instructions:
1. Preheat oven to 375°F (190°C).
2. Toss sliced fennel with olive oil, lemon juice, salt, and thyme.
3. Spread on a baking sheet and roast for 25 minutes until caramelized.

Nutritional Information
(Per Serving):
Calories: 80 | **Protein:** 2g
Carbs: 10g | **Fat:** 4g | **Fiber:** 1.9g

Sautéed Swiss Chard with Garlic & Pine Nuts

Prep: 5 min | **Cook:** 10 min | **Serv:** 4
Ingredients:
- 2 cups Swiss chard, chopped
- 1 tbsp olive oil
- 1 garlic clove, minced
- 2 tbsp pine nuts
- 1/4 tsp sea salt

Instructions:
1. Heat olive oil in a pan over medium heat.
2. Add garlic and sauté for 30 seconds.
3. Add Swiss chard and cook for 5 minutes until wilted.
4. Stir in pine nuts and season with salt.

Nutritional Information
(Per Serving):
Calories: 100 | **Protein:** 3g
Carbs: 8g | **Fat:** 7g | **Fiber:** 0.5g

Roasted Red Onion with Balsamic & Thyme

Prep: 5 min | **Cook:** 20 min | **Serv:** 4
Ingredients:
- 2 red onions, sliced
- 1 tbsp olive oil
- 1 tbsp balsamic vinegar
- 1/2 tsp dried thyme
- 1/4 tsp sea salt

Instructions:
1. Preheat oven to 375°F (190°C).
2. Toss sliced red onions with olive oil, balsamic vinegar, thyme, and sea salt.
3. Roast for 20 minutes until caramelized.

Nutritional Information
(Per Serving):
Calories: 80 | **Protein:** 1g
Carbs: 10g | **Fat:** 4g | **Fiber:** 1g

Warm Mediterranean Tomato & Olive Salad

Prep: 5 min | **Cook:** 10 min | **Serv:** 4
Ingredients:
- 1 cup cherry tomatoes, halved
- 1/4 cup Kalamata olives, chopped
- 1 tbsp olive oil
- 1/2 tsp dried oregano
- 1 tbsp lemon juice

Instructions:
1. Heat olive oil in a pan over medium heat.
2. Add cherry tomatoes and cook for 5 minutes until softened.
3. Stir in olives, oregano, and lemon juice.
4. Serve warm as a flavorful side dish.

Nutritional Information
(Per Serving):
Calories: 100 | **Protein:** 2g
Carbs: 8g | **Fat:** 7g | **Fiber:** 1g

Roasted Eggplant & Garlic Mash

Prep: 5 min | **Cook:** 20 min | **Serv:** 2
Ingredients:
- 1 small eggplant, diced
- 1 teaspoon olive oil
- 1 garlic clove, minced
- ¼ teaspoon cumin
- ½ teaspoon lemon juice

Instructions:
1. Preheat oven to 375°F (190°C).
2. Toss eggplant with olive oil and cumin, then roast for 20 minutes.
3. Mash roasted eggplant with garlic and lemon juice before serving.

Nutritional Information (Per Serving):
Calories: 80 | **Protein:** 2g
Carbs: 9g | **Fat:** 4g | **Fiber:** 3g

Mediterranean Roasted Peppers & Olives

Prep: 5 min | **Cook:** 12 min | **Serv:** 2
Ingredients:
- 1 red bell pepper, sliced
- ½ cup mixed olives
- 1 teaspoon olive oil
- ½ teaspoon oregano
- ¼ teaspoon black pepper

Instructions:
1. Preheat oven to 375°F (190°C).
2. Toss bell pepper slices with olive oil, oregano, and black pepper.
3. Roast for 12 minutes.
4. Mix with olives before serving.

Nutritional Information (Per Serving):
Calories: 110 | **Protein:** 2g
Carbs: 8g | **Fat:** 8g | **Fiber:** 3g

Roasted Pumpkin with Cinnamon & Honey

Prep: 5 min | **Cook:** 20 min | **Serv:** 4
Ingredients:
- 2 cups pumpkin, diced
- 1 tbsp olive oil
- 1 tbsp honey
- 1/2 tsp ground cinnamon
- 1/4 tsp sea salt

Instructions:
1. Preheat oven to 375°F (190°C).
2. Toss pumpkin cubes with olive oil, honey, cinnamon, and sea salt.
3. Spread on a baking sheet and roast for 20 minutes until tender.

Nutritional Information (Per Serving):
Calories: | **Protein:** 2g
Carbs: 15g | **Fat:** 5g | **Fiber:** 0.8g

Air-Fried Cauliflower with Paprika

Prep: 5 min | **Cook:** 12 min | **Serv:** 2
Ingredients:
- 1 cup cauliflower florets
- 1 teaspoon olive oil
- ½ teaspoon smoked paprika
- ¼ teaspoon garlic powder
- ¼ teaspoon sea salt

Instructions:
1. Preheat air fryer to 375°F (190°C).
2. Toss cauliflower with olive oil, smoked paprika, garlic powder, and sea salt.
3. Air-fry for 12 minutes, shaking halfway through.

Nutritional Information (Per Serving):
Calories: 85 | **Protein:** 3g
Carbs: 9g | **Fat:** 4g | **Fiber:** 3g

Grilled Zucchini with Basil & Parmesan

Prep: 5 min | **Cook:** 8 min | **Serv:** 2
Ingredients:
- 1 small zucchini, sliced
- 1 teaspoon olive oil
- ½ teaspoon dried basil
- 2 tablespoons grated Parmesan cheese
- ¼ teaspoon black pepper

Instructions:
1. Preheat grill to medium heat.
2. Toss zucchini with olive oil, basil, and black pepper.
3. Grill for 4 minutes on each side.
4. Sprinkle with Parmesan before serving.

Nutritional Information (Per Serving):
Calories: 100 | **Protein:** 5g
Carbs: 6g | **Fat:** 7g | **Fiber:** 2g

Sautéed Mushrooms with Thyme

Prep: 5 min | **Cook:** 10 min | **Serv:** 2
Ingredients:
- 1 cup sliced mushrooms
- 1 teaspoon olive oil
- ½ teaspoon dried thyme
- ¼ teaspoon sea salt
- ¼ teaspoon black pepper

Instructions:
1. Heat olive oil in a pan over medium heat.
2. Add mushrooms, thyme, salt, and black pepper.
3. Sauté for 10 minutes until tender.

Nutritional Information (Per Serving):
Calories: 90 | **Protein:** 4g
Carbs: 7g | **Fat:** 5g | **Fiber:** 2g

Sweet Mediterranean Treats

Honey & Orange Yogurt Parfait

Prep: 5 min | **Cook:** 0 min | **Serv:** 2

Ingredients:
- 1 cup Greek yogurt (low-fat)
- 1 teaspoon honey
- ½ teaspoon orange zest
- ¼ teaspoon cinnamon
- ¼ cup chopped almonds

Instructions:
1. In a bowl, mix Greek yogurt, honey, orange zest, and cinnamon.
2. Divide between two serving bowls.
3. Sprinkle with chopped almonds and serve immediately.

Nutritional Information (Per Serving):
Calories: 150 | **Protein:** 10g
Carbs: 14g | **Fat:** 5g | **Fiber:** 2g

Baked Cinnamon Apple Slices

Prep: 5 min | **Cook:** 15 min | **Serv:** 2

Ingredients:
- 1 large apple, sliced
- ½ teaspoon cinnamon
- 1 teaspoon honey
- ¼ teaspoon nutmeg
- ½ teaspoon lemon juice

Instructions:
1. Preheat oven to 375°F (190°C).
2. Toss apple slices with cinnamon, honey, nutmeg, and lemon juice.
3. Arrange on a baking sheet and bake for 15 minutes.
4. Serve warm.

Nutritional Information (Per Serving):
Calories: 120 | **Protein:** 1g
Carbs: 30g | **Fat:** 1g | **Fiber:** 5g

Dark Chocolate & Pistachio Bites

Prep: 5 min | **Cook:** 0 min | **Serv:** 6

Ingredients:
- ¼ cup dark chocolate (85% cocoa), melted
- 2 tablespoons pistachios, chopped
- 1 teaspoon honey
- ½ teaspoon vanilla extract
- ¼ teaspoon sea salt

Instructions:
1. Melt dark chocolate and stir in honey and vanilla extract.
2. Spoon small circles of the mixture onto parchment paper.
3. Sprinkle with chopped pistachios and sea salt.
4. Let set in the fridge for 15 minutes.

Nutritional Information (Per Serving):
Calories: 80 | **Protein:** 2g
Carbs: 8g | **Fat:** 5g | **Fiber:** 2g

Mediterranean Almond & Date Energy Balls

Prep: 5 min | **Cook:** 0 min | **Serv:** 6 balls

Ingredients:
- ½ cup almonds
- ¼ cup dates, pitted
- ½ teaspoon cinnamon
- ½ teaspoon orange zest
- ½ teaspoon vanilla extract

Instructions:
1. Blend all ingredients in a food processor until a sticky dough forms.
2. Roll into small balls and refrigerate for 10 minutes.
3. Serve chilled, optionally rolling them in shredded coconut or crushed almonds for extra texture.

Nutritional Information (Per Serving):
Calories: 90 | **Protein:** 2g
Carbs: 12g | **Fat:** 4g | **Fiber:** 2g

Apricot & Sesame Bites

Prep: 10 min | **Cook:** 0 min | **Serv:** 6
Ingredients:
- 1/2 cup dried apricots
- 1/4 cup walnuts
- 1 tbsp sesame seeds
- 1 tbsp tahini
- 1/2 tsp orange zest

Instructions:
1. Blend dried apricots, walnuts, sesame seeds, tahini, and orange zest in a food processor until a sticky dough forms.
2. Roll into small bites and coat with extra sesame seeds.
3. Refrigerate for at least 30 minutes before serving.

Nutritional Information (Per Serving):
Calories: 110 | **Protein:** 3g
Carbs: 15g | **Fat:** 5g | **Fiber:** 1.2g

Chia & Coconut Pudding

Prep: 5 min | **Cook:** 0 min | **Serv:** 4
Ingredients:
- 1/4 cup chia seeds
- 1 cup unsweetened almond milk
- 1 tbsp honey
- 1/4 cup shredded coconut
- 1/2 tsp vanilla extract

Instructions:
1. Mix all ingredients in a bowl.
2. Let sit in the refrigerator for at least 2 hours until thickened.
3. Serve chilled, optionally topped with extra shredded coconut, fresh berries, or a drizzle of honey for added sweetness.

Nutritional Information (Per Serving):
Calories: 160 | **Protein:** 5g
Carbs: 12g | **Fat:** 9g | **Fiber:** 4.3g

Roasted Pears with Cinnamon & Almonds

Prep: 5 min | **Cook:** 15 min | **Serv:** 2

Ingredients:
- 1 large pear, halved
- 1 teaspoon honey
- ½ teaspoon cinnamon
- ¼ teaspoon vanilla extract
- 1 tablespoon sliced almonds

Instructions:
1. Preheat oven to 375°F (190°C).
2. Drizzle pear halves with honey and vanilla extract.
3. Sprinkle with cinnamon and top with almonds.
4. Roast for 15 minutes.

Nutritional Information (Per Serving):
Calories: 130 | **Protein:** 2g
Carbs: 30g | **Fat:** 3g | **Fiber:** 4g

Orange & Olive Oil Mini Muffins

Prep: 5 min | **Cook:** 12 min | **Serv:** 4

Ingredients:
- ½ cup whole wheat flour
- ½ teaspoon baking powder
- 1 teaspoon olive oil
- ½ teaspoon orange zest
- 1 teaspoon honey

Instructions:
1. Preheat oven to 350°F (175°C).
2. Mix all ingredients into a smooth batter.
3. Divide into a mini muffin tin and bake for 12 minutes.
4. Let cool before serving.

Nutritional Information (Per Serving - 2 muffins):
Calories: 120 | **Protein:** 3g
Carbs: 18g | **Fat:** 3g | **Fiber:** 2g

Pomegranate & Honey Glazed Figs

Prep: 5 min | **Cook:** 10 min | **Serv:** 4
Ingredients:
- 4 fresh figs, halved
- 1 tbsp honey
- 1 tbsp pomegranate juice
- 1/2 tsp ground cinnamon
- 2 tbsp chopped pistachios

Instructions:
1. Preheat oven to 375°F (190°C).
2. Arrange fig halves in a baking dish.
3. Drizzle with honey and pomegranate juice, then sprinkle with cinnamon.
4. Bake for 10 minutes until caramelized.
5. Garnish with chopped pistachios before serving.

Nutritional Information (Per Serving):
Calories: 120 | **Protein:** 2g
Carbs: 20g | **Fat:** 4g | **Fiber:** 2.3g

Dark Chocolate-Dipped Apricots

Prep: 5 min | **Cook:** 0 min | **Serv:** 6
Ingredients:
- 6 dried apricots
- ¼ cup dark chocolate (85% cocoa), melted
- ½ teaspoon coconut oil
- ¼ teaspoon sea salt
- 1 teaspoon crushed almonds

Instructions:
1. Melt dark chocolate with coconut oil.
2. Dip each apricot halfway into the chocolate.
3. Sprinkle with sea salt and crushed almonds.
4. Place on parchment paper and refrigerate for 10 minutes.

Nutritional Information (Per Serving):
Calories: 90 | **Protein:** 1g
Carbs: 14g | **Fat:** 4g | **Fiber:** 2g

Honey & Cinnamon Baked Apples

Prep: 5 min | **Cook:** 15 min | **Serv:** 2

Ingredients:
- 1 large apple, cored
- 1 teaspoon honey
- ¼ teaspoon cinnamon
- 1 tablespoon chopped walnuts
- ¼ teaspoon lemon zest

Instructions:
1. Preheat oven to 375°F (190°C).
2. Arrange apple slices in a baking dish.
3. Drizzle with honey and sprinkle with cinnamon.
4. Bake for 15 minutes.
5. Top with walnuts and lemon zest before serving.

Nutritional Information (Per Serving):
Calories: 140 | **Protein:** 1g
Carbs: 28g | **Fat:** 4g | **Fiber:** 4g

Dark Chocolate & Almond Energy Bites

Prep: 5 min | **Cook:** 0 min | **Serv:** 4

Ingredients:
- ½ cup almonds, chopped
- ¼ cup dark chocolate chips
- 1 teaspoon honey
- ½ teaspoon vanilla extract
- ¼ teaspoon cinnamon

Instructions:
1. Melt dark chocolate chips in a microwave-safe bowl.
2. Stir in chopped almonds, honey, vanilla extract, and cinnamon.
3. Form small balls and place them on a parchment-lined tray.
4. Refrigerate for 15 minutes before serving.

Nutritional Information (Per Serving - 2 bites):
Calories: 150 | **Protein:** 3g
Carbs: 10g | **Fat:** 10g | **Fiber:** 2g

Greek Yogurt & Honey Parfait

Prep: 5 min | **Cook:** 0 min | **Serv:** 2
Ingredients:
- 1 cup Greek yogurt (low-fat)
- 1 teaspoon honey
- ¼ teaspoon cinnamon
- ¼ cup fresh berries
- 1 tablespoon sliced almonds

Instructions:
1. Divide Greek yogurt into two serving bowls.
2. Drizzle with honey and sprinkle with cinnamon.
3. Top with fresh berries and sliced almonds.
4. Serve immediately, optionally layering the ingredients for a visually appealing parfait.

Nutritional Information (Per Serving):
Calories: 160 | **Protein:** 10g
Carbs: 18g | **Fat:** 5g | **Fiber:** 2g

Pomegranate & Dark Chocolate Clusters

Prep: 5 min | **Cook:** 5 min | **Serv:** 4
Ingredients:
- ½ cup pomegranate seeds
- ¼ cup dark chocolate, melted
- 1 teaspoon honey
- ¼ teaspoon sea salt
- ¼ teaspoon orange zest

Instructions:
1. Line a tray with parchment paper.
2. Mix pomegranate seeds with honey and orange zest.
3. Spoon small clusters onto the parchment paper.
4. Drizzle with melted dark chocolate and sprinkle with sea salt.
5. Refrigerate for 15 minutes before serving.

Nutritional Information (Per Serving - 2 clusters):
Calories: 130 | **Protein:** 2g
Carbs: 18g | **Fat:** 6g | **Fiber:** 3g

Almond & Fig Bars

Prep: 5 min | **Cook:** 0 min | **Serv:** 4

Ingredients:
- ½ cup dried figs, chopped
- ¼ cup almonds
- 1 teaspoon honey
- ¼ teaspoon cinnamon
- ¼ teaspoon vanilla extract

Instructions:
1. Blend dried figs, almonds, honey, cinnamon, and vanilla extract in a food processor until a sticky dough forms.
2. Press mixture into a lined dish and refrigerate for 15 minutes.
3. Slice into bars and serve.

Nutritional Information (Per Serving - 1 bar):
Calories: 140 | **Protein:** 3g
Carbs: 22g | **Fat:** 5g | **Fiber:** 3g

Citrus & Honey Drizzled Ricotta

Prep: 5 min | **Cook:** 0 min | **Serv:** 2

Ingredients:
- ½ cup ricotta cheese (low-fat)
- 1 teaspoon honey
- ¼ teaspoon cinnamon
- 1 teaspoon orange zest
- 1 tablespoon chopped pistachios

Instructions:
1. Divide ricotta cheese into two bowls.
2. Drizzle with honey and sprinkle with cinnamon.
3. Garnish with orange zest and pistachios before serving.

Nutritional Information (Per Serving):
Calories: 150 | **Protein:** 7g
Carbs: 12g | **Fat:** 7g | **Fiber:** 1g

Coconut & Date Truffles

Prep: 5 min | **Cook:** 0 min | **Serv:** 4

Ingredients:
- ½ cup dates, pitted
- ¼ cup shredded coconut
- 1 teaspoon honey
- ¼ teaspoon cinnamon
- ¼ teaspoon vanilla extract

Instructions:
1. Blend dates, shredded coconut, honey, cinnamon, and vanilla extract in a food processor.
2. Form into small truffle balls.
3. Roll in extra shredded coconut and refrigerate for 15 minutes before serving.

Nutritional Information (Per Serving - 2 truffles):
Calories: 140 | **Protein:** 2g
Carbs: 22g | **Fat:** 5g | **Fiber:** 3g

Chilled Watermelon & Mint Delight

Prep: 5 min | **Cook:** 0 min | **Serv:** 2

Ingredients:
- 2 cups watermelon cubes
- 1 teaspoon honey
- ½ teaspoon lime juice
- 4 fresh mint leaves, chopped
- ¼ teaspoon sea salt

Instructions:
1. Toss watermelon cubes with honey, lime juice, and chopped mint.
2. Sprinkle with sea salt.
3. Serve chilled.

Nutritional Information (Per Serving):
Calories: 90 | **Protein:** 2g
Carbs: 20g | **Fat:** 1g | **Fiber:** 1g

Honey & Almond Clusters

Prep: 5 min | **Cook:** 10 min | **Serv:** 10

Ingredients:
- 1/2 cup raw almonds, chopped
- 1 tbsp honey
- 1 tbsp sesame seeds
- 1/2 tsp ground cinnamon
- 1 tbsp orange zest

Instructions:
1. Preheat oven to 350°F (175°C).
2. In a bowl, mix almonds, honey, sesame seeds, and cinnamon.
3. Place small clusters on a parchment-lined baking sheet.
4. Bake for 10 minutes until golden brown.
5. Let cool and garnish with orange zest.

Nutritional Information (Per Serving):
Calories: 90 | **Protein:** 3g
Carbs: 8g | **Fat:** 6g | **Fiber** 1g

Grilled Peaches with Ricotta & Honey

Prep: 5 min | **Cook:** 5 min | **Serv:** 4

Ingredients:
- 2 peaches, halved and pitted
- 1/2 cup ricotta cheese
- 1 tbsp honey
- 1 tbsp chopped hazelnuts
- 1/2 tsp ground cinnamon

Instructions:
1. Heat a grill pan over medium heat.
2. Grill peaches cut-side down for 3 minutes until caramelized.
3. Top with ricotta, drizzle with honey, and sprinkle with hazelnuts and cinnamon.

Nutritional Information (Per Serving):
Calories: 150 | **Protein:** 5g
Carbs: 18g | **Fat:** 6g | **Fiber:** 1.6g

Simple Mediterranean Meal Plans: 2000 Days of Inspiration

Eating well doesn't have to be complicated. With just a little planning and a well-stocked Mediterranean pantry, you can enjoy **delicious, satisfying meals using only five ingredients**. This chapter provides you with a structured **4-week meal plan**, carefully designed to bring balance, variety, and **1000 days of Mediterranean inspiration** into your daily life.

The Power of a 4-Week Mediterranean Meal Plan

The **Mediterranean diet** is all about **fresh ingredients, balance, and simplicity**. This **4-week plan** ensures you get a mix of **lean proteins, healthy fats, whole grains, and fresh produce** while keeping meal prep effortless. Each meal follows the **5-ingredient philosophy**, proving that **healthy eating doesn't require long grocery lists or complex recipes**.

By following this meal plan, you'll enjoy:
- ✓ **Quick & Easy Meals** – Most recipes take **30 minutes or less**, perfect for busy schedules.
- ✓ **Nutrient-Dense Ingredients** – A focus on **wholesome, minimally processed foods** to fuel your body.
- ✓ **Endless Variety** – With **124+ recipes**, you can rotate meals and enjoy fresh flavors every day.
- ✓ **1000 Days of Inspiration** – This **4-week cycle** can be **repeated, customized, or shuffled**, giving you **years of Mediterranean-inspired meal planning**.

How to Use This Meal Plan

This plan provides **breakfast, lunch, snacks, dinner, and desserts** to keep your meals balanced and enjoyable. Feel free to:
- ✓ **Swap meals** based on availability or preference.
- ✓ **Adjust portions** to fit your dietary needs.
- ✓ **Batch-cook or prep ahead** to save time during the week.

Whether you're new to the Mediterranean diet or looking for **a structured, stress-free way to eat healthy**, this **4-week plan** will set you up for **long-term success**.

Week 1

Day	Breakfast	Lunch	Snack	Dinner	Dessert
Day 1	Greek Yogurt with Chia, Almonds & Berries (p.9)	Mediterranean Chickpea & Cucumber Salad (p.20)	Zucchini Chips with Garlic & Oregano (p.31)	Lemon Garlic Shrimp with Zucchini Noodles (p.40)	Dark Chocolate & Almond Energy Bites (p.65)
Day 2	Mediterranean Chia Seed Pudding (p.10)	Roasted Beet & Walnut Salad (p.20)	Stuffed Mini Peppers with Hummus (p.31)	Garlic & Herb Grilled Chicken Breasts (p.43)	Greek Yogurt & Honey Parfait (p.66)
Day 3	Mediterranean Tomato & Feta Scramble (p.9)	Avocado & Cherry Tomato Salad (p.19)	Baked Feta with Tomatoes (p.29)	Mediterranean Baked Cod with Lemon & Herbs (p.42)	Pomegranate & Honey Glazed Figs (p.64)
Day 4	Avocado & Egg Mediterranean Wrap (p.11)	Warm Lentil & Carrot Salad (p.25)	Roasted Red Pepper & Walnut Dip (p.33)	Mediterranean Stuffed Bell Peppers (p.42)	Baked Cinnamon Apple Slices (p.60)
Day 5	Cinnamon-Spiced Quinoa Breakfast Bowl (p.14)	Cucumber & Dill Yogurt Salad (p.19)	Lemon & Herb Marinated Feta Cubes (p.34)	Greek-Style Baked Chicken Thighs (p.45)	Apricot & Sesame Bites (p.62)
Day 6	Air-Fried Zucchini & Egg Frittata (p.10)	Roasted Cauliflower & Chickpea Salad (p.24)	Eggplant & Chickpea Patties (p.37)	Balsamic Glazed Chicken & Mushrooms (p.46)	Dark Chocolate & Pistachio Bites (p.61)
Day 7	Cottage Cheese & Fig Bowl (p.15)	Chickpea & Caper Mediterranean Salad (p.28)	Stuffed Dates with Almond Butter (p.35)	Roasted Eggplant & Tomato Stew (p.44)	Grilled Peaches with Ricotta & Honey (p.69)

Week 2

Day	Breakfast	Lunch	Snack	Dinner	Dessert
Day 1	Mediterranean Lemon & Honey Porridge (p.18)	Radish & Fennel Crunch Salad (p.26)	Marinated Cherry Tomatoes with Basil (p.36)	Mediterranean Duck with Cherry Sauce (p.47)	Pomegranate & Dark Chocolate Clusters (p.66)
Day 2	Scrambled Eggs with Sun-Dried Tomatoes & Basil (p.16)	Roasted Pepper & Feta Salad (p.21)	Air-Fried Stuffed Mushrooms (p.38)	Spiced Turkey & Zucchini Skillet (p.47)	Citrus & Honey Drizzled Ricotta (p.67)
Day 3	Greek Yogurt & Pistachio Bowl (p.16)	Arugula & Roasted Red Pepper Salad (p.25)	Zesty Carrot & Cumin Dip (p.38)	Roasted Eggplant & Tahini Bowl (p.48)	Chia & Coconut Pudding (p.62)
Day 4	Mediterranean Chia Pudding with Berries (p.12)	Cabbage & Apple Slaw (p.21)	Marinated Cherry Tomatoes with Basil (p.36)	Garlic & Herb Grilled Chicken Breasts (p.43)	Dark Chocolate & Almond Energy Bites (p.65)
Day 5	Mediterranean Almond Flour Pancakes (p.11)	Roasted Cauliflower & Chickpea Salad (p.24)	Zucchini Fritters with Dill (p.39)	Roasted Eggplant & Tomato Stew (p.44)	Chia & Coconut Pudding (p.62)
Day 6	Cinnamon-Spiced Quinoa Breakfast Bowl (p.14)	Warm Lentil & Carrot Salad (p.25)	Air-Fried Zucchini Parmesan Bites (p.35)	Mediterranean Baked Cod with Lemon & Herbs (p.42)	Pomegranate & Honey Glazed Figs (p.64)
Day 7	Scrambled Eggs with Sun-Dried Tomatoes & Basil (p.16)	Scrambled Eggs with Sun-Dried Tomatoes & Basil (p.16)	Grilled Mushroom & Thyme Bites (p.33)	One-Pan Mediterranean Turkey Skillet (p.41)	Honey & Orange Yogurt Parfait (p.60)

Week 3

Day	Breakfast	Lunch	Snack	Dinner	Dessert
Day 1	Baked Ricotta with Honey & Nuts (p.17)	Arugula & Walnut Salad with Lemon Zest (p.22)	Fava Bean & Mint Dip (p.30)	Chickpea & Spinach Stir-Fry (p.43)	Coconut & Date Truffles (p.68)
Day 2	Air-Fried Sweet Potato & Egg Hash (p.14)	Roasted Carrot & Chickpea Salad (p.27)	Roasted Red Pepper & Garlic Dip (p.39)	Mediterranean Lentil & Spinach Stir-Fry (p.41)	Pomegranate & Honey Glazed Figs (p.64)
Day 3	Mediterranean Fig & Almond Smoothie (p.13)	Cucumber, Dill & Feta Salad (p.27)	Air-Fried Zucchini Parmesan Bites (p.35)	Grilled Salmon with Olive Tapenade (p.46)	Honey & Orange Yogurt Parfait (p.60)
Day 4	Dark Chocolate & Walnut Overnight Oats (p.18)	Warm Mediterranean Tomato & Olive Salad (p.56)	Stuffed Grape Leaves with Lemon & Herbs (p.36)	Mediterranean Baked Cod with Lemon & Herbs (p.42)	Chilled Watermelon & Mint Delight (p.68)
Day 5	Cucumber & Labneh Breakfast Bowl (p.12)	Avocado & Roasted Tomato Salad (p.24)	Air-Fried Eggplant Chips with Lemon Zest (p.32)	One-Pan Mediterranean Turkey Skillet (p.41)	Almond & Fig Bars (p.67)
Day 6	Air-Fried Mediterranean Apple Rings (p.13)	Roasted Brussels Sprouts with Balsamic Glaze (p.54)	Grilled Mushroom & Thyme Bites (p.33)	Garlic & Herb Turkey Meatballs (p.40)	Honey & Almond Clusters (p.69)
Day 7	Scrambled Eggs with Sun-Dried Tomatoes & Basil (p.16)	Chickpea & Caper Mediterranean Salad (p.28)	Marinated Artichoke & Olive Skewers (p.32)	Mediterranean Stuffed Bell Peppers (p.42)	Dark Chocolate-Dipped Apricots (p.64)

Week 4

Day	Breakfast	Lunch	Snack	Dinner	Dessert
Day 1	Mediterranean Lemon & Honey Porridge (p.18)	Grilled Zucchini & Halloumi Salad (p.28)	Spinach & Cheese Bites (p.34)	Mediterranean Lentil & Spinach Stir-Fry (p.41)	Roasted Pears with Cinnamon & Almonds (p.63)
Day 2	Cottage Cheese & Fig Bowl (p.15)	Roasted Pepper & Feta Salad (p.21)	Zesty Carrot & Cumin Dip (p.38)	Spiced Turkey & Zucchini Skillet (p.47)	Dark Chocolate & Pistachio Bites (p.61)
Day 3	Mediterranean Almond Flour Pancakes (p.11)	Cabbage & Carrot Slaw with Lemon Dressing (p.22)	Crispy Zucchini & Parmesan Bites (p.37)	Garlic Lemon Shrimp with Zucchini Noodles (p.44)	Pomegranate & Dark Chocolate Clusters (p.66)
Day 4	Greek Yogurt & Pistachio Bowl (p.16)	Roasted Eggplant & Garlic Mash (p.57)	Stuffed Dates with Almond Butter (p.35)	Greek-Style Baked Chicken Thighs (p.45)	Citrus & Honey Drizzled Ricotta (p.67)
Day 5	Dark Chocolate & Walnut Overnight Oats (p.18)	Zucchini & Mint Salad with Yogurt Dressing (p.23)	Air-Fried Stuffed Mushrooms (p.38)	Roasted Eggplant & Tahini Bowl (p.48)	Apricot & Sesame Bites (p.62)
Day 6	Avocado & Egg Mediterranean Wrap (p.11)	Roasted Cherry Tomatoes with Basil (p.53)	Air-Fried Zucchini Parmesan Bites (p.35)	Garlic & Herb Grilled Chicken Breasts (p.43)	Orange & Olive Oil Mini Muffins (p.63)
Day 7	Baked Ricotta with Honey & Nuts (p.17)	Spinach & Roasted Almond Salad (p.26)	Fava Bean & Mint Dip (p.30)	Mediterranean Duck with Cherry Sauce (p.47)	Honey & Cinnamon Baked Apples (p.65)

Tips for Quick Meal Prep

Meal prepping is key to **saving time and making healthy eating effortless**. Here are some simple strategies to help you stay on track without spending hours in the kitchen.

1. Batch Cook Staples
   Many Mediterranean ingredients can be **prepared in advance** and used throughout the week.
   - **Cooked Quinoa or Lentils** → Store in an airtight container and use in salads, sides, or main dishes.
   - **Roasted Vegetables** → Roast bell peppers, zucchini, eggplant, and carrots in bulk for easy meal additions.
   - **Grilled Chicken or Fish** → Prepare a few portions in advance for quick dinners or protein-packed lunches.
2. Pre-Chop Fresh Ingredients
   Chopping vegetables ahead of time **cuts down on prep work** during busy weekdays.
   - **Cucumbers, tomatoes, and bell peppers** → Store in separate containers to mix into salads or side dishes.
   - **Leafy greens like spinach or arugula** → Wash and store in an airtight container with a paper towel to absorb moisture.
   - **Herbs like parsley, cilantro, and basil** → Chop and store in a small container for easy seasoning.
3. Make Dressings & Sauces in Advance
   Mediterranean dishes often rely on **simple yet flavorful dressings**. Prepare these ahead of time and **store them in jars** for quick drizzling over meals.
   Try making:
   - **Lemon & Olive Oil Dressing** (olive oil + lemon juice + garlic + oregano)
   - **Tahini Sauce** (tahini + lemon juice + garlic + water)
   - **Greek Yogurt & Cucumber Sauce** (Greek yogurt + grated cucumber + garlic + dill)
4. Use Smart Storage Solutions
   Keeping your ingredients **organized and easy to access** ensures you can cook meals quickly without stress.
   - **Label and date all prepped ingredients** to keep track of freshness.
   - **Store grains and legumes in airtight containers** to prevent moisture and pests.
   - **Keep snacks like nuts, dried fruit, and energy bites in small jars** for quick grab-and-go options.
5. Freeze for Convenience
   Some ingredients and dishes **freeze well**, allowing you to prepare meals in bulk and store them for later use.
   - **Cooked lentils, chickpeas, and beans** → Freeze in portioned containers for easy meal additions.
   - **Homemade soups and stews** → Make extra and freeze individual servings for quick dinners.
   - **Baked goods like almond flour muffins or pistachio bites** → Store in the freezer for a quick snack.

Conclusion

Throughout this cookbook, we've explored the **simplicity, flavor, and health benefits** of the *5-ingredient Mediterranean diet*. By embracing a minimalist approach to cooking—focusing on fresh, high-quality ingredients—you've discovered that **healthy meals don't have to be complicated**. With just five ingredients, you can create dishes that are not only easy to prepare but also deeply satisfying and rich in nutrients.

The Mediterranean diet is more than just a way of eating; it's a **lifestyle rooted in balance, wellness, and enjoyment**. It's about **savoring every meal, celebrating fresh and wholesome ingredients, and nourishing both body and soul**. Whether you're whipping up a quick breakfast, a satisfying salad, or a deliciously simple main course, the recipes in this book prove that eating well can be both effortless and enjoyable.

The Beauty of Simplicity

One of the biggest takeaways from this cookbook is that **simplicity leads to success**. Cooking doesn't have to be overwhelming—when you strip recipes down to their core elements, you unlock the **true essence of Mediterranean flavors**.

By focusing on just five ingredients, you've learned to:
- **Save time** in the kitchen while still creating nourishing meals.
- **Reduce waste** by using fresh, versatile ingredients efficiently.
- **Enjoy bold, natural flavors** without relying on processed foods.
- **Adopt a sustainable approach** to healthy eating that's both practical and fulfilling.

This journey is about **more than just recipes**—it's about embracing a new way of thinking about food. Cooking with fewer ingredients doesn't mean sacrificing flavor or variety; it means **choosing wisely, cooking mindfully, and savoring every bite**.

Embracing the Mediterranean Lifestyle Beyond the Kitchen

The Mediterranean way of life extends far beyond what's on your plate. It's a **holistic approach to well-being**, blending good food with **movement, mindfulness, and meaningful connections**.

Here's how you can take the spirit of Mediterranean living beyond the kitchen:

1. Make Mealtime an Experience

   In Mediterranean cultures, meals are not rushed—they are meant to be **shared, savored, and enjoyed**. Whether dining alone or with loved ones, make an effort to:
   - **Sit down at the table** and be present with your food.
   - **Share meals with family or friends** whenever possible.
   - **Savor each bite** rather than eating on the go.

   By turning meals into **intentional moments**, you naturally develop a healthier relationship with food and appreciation for simple pleasures.

2. Move Naturally & Joyfully

   The Mediterranean lifestyle isn't about intense workouts—it's about **moving in ways that feel natural and enjoyable**. Instead of rigid exercise routines, try:
   - **Taking daily walks**—preferably outdoors.
   - **Practicing yoga or stretching** to stay flexible and strong.
   - **Engaging in active hobbies** like cycling, dancing, or gardening.

Movement should feel like **a celebration of life, not a chore**.
3. Connect with Your Community

Mediterranean cultures thrive on **social connection**. Spending time with others is as nourishing as the food itself.
- **Enjoy conversations** over a meal with loved ones.
- **Visit local farmers' markets** and engage with your community.
- **Share your cooking**—host a Mediterranean-inspired dinner night.

Prioritizing relationships and fostering a sense of belonging **boosts both happiness and longevity**.

4. Find Joy in Slowing Down

The Mediterranean approach to life values **slowing down and appreciating the present moment**. Instead of rushing from task to task, embrace:
- **Mindfulness**—whether while eating, walking, or simply breathing.
- **Time outdoors**—soaking in sunlight and fresh air.
- **Simple pleasures**—reading, journaling, or listening to music.

A Mediterranean life is one that's **balanced, joyful, and deeply fulfilling**.

Final Words: Your Mediterranean Journey Starts Now

As you close this cookbook, remember that the **Mediterranean diet is not a restrictive plan—it's a lifestyle of abundance**. It's about enjoying fresh, wholesome food, moving your body, connecting with others, and **making every meal an opportunity to nourish yourself**.

By cooking with just **five simple ingredients**, you've unlocked a world of **flavor, nutrition, and effortless meals**. Now, take what you've learned and **make it your own**—whether that means meal prepping for a busy week, hosting a Mediterranean-inspired gathering, or simply enjoying a fresh, homemade salad.

The Mediterranean way is about **savoring life one meal at a time**—and now, you're fully equipped to do just that.